IMAGES OF WAR

ARMOURED WARFARE
IN THE
KOREAN WAR

Tank warfare in Korea was something completely new because of the geography involved. (*US DoD*)

IMAGES OF WAR

ARMOURED WARFARE
IN THE
KOREAN WAR

RARE PHOTOGRAPHS FROM
WARTIME ARCHIVES

Anthony Tucker-Jones

Pen & Sword
MILITARY

First published in Great Britain in 2012
and reprinted in 2021 by
PEN & SWORD MILITARY
an imprint of
Pen & Sword Books Ltd,
47 Church Street,
Barnsley,
South Yorkshire
S70 2AS

A CIP record for this book is available from the British Library.

ISBN 978 1 84884 580 0

Typeset by Chic Media Ltd

Printed and bound by CPI Group (UK) Ltd, Croydon, CR0 4YY

Pen & Sword Books Ltd incorporates the Imprints of
Pen & Sword Aviation, Pen & Sword Family History, Pen & Sword Maritime, Pen & Sword Military, Pen & Sword Discovery, Wharncliffe Local History, Wharncliffe True Crime, Wharncliffe Transport, Pen & Sword Select, Pen & Sword Military Classics, Leo Cooper, The Praetorian Press, Remember When, Seaforth Publishing and Frontline Publishing.

For a complete list of Pen & Sword titles please contact
Pen & Sword Books Limited
47 Church Street, Barnsley, South Yorkshire, S70 2AS, England
E-mail: enquiries@pen-and-sword.co.uk
Website: www.pen-and-sword.co.uk

Contents

Introduction

After the Second World War many military analysts thought that the only place significant armoured warfare was likely to take place again was in central Europe. However, the Korean War was to witness the use of large numbers of armoured fighting vehicles, though their role would be very different to that of the 1940s. The North Korean 'Blitzkrieg' was to be very short-lived.

The landscape of Korea is far from suited to modern mechanised warfare. At the time of the Korean War much of the countryside was forested, while the Taebaek Mountains form a central spine near the east coast. Although the Korean peninsula is about 450 miles long, it only averages about 160 miles wide creating a very narrow fighting front.

The country's rugged mountains, narrow passes, steep valleys and waterlogged fields were clearly not ideal tank country. In fact, tanks were not to be pitted against each other in any great numbers. Nonetheless, armour did play an effective if unorthodox part in the swiftly moving campaign of the first year.

In contrast, the geography of northern Korea was tailor-made for guerrilla warfare. It favoured the lightly armed North Korean and Chinese forces, especially in the case of the latter, the strength of which lay in vast numbers of hardy, self-sufficient infantry. For China manpower was never a problem.

Following the North Korean invasion of the South in the summer of 1950, the North Korean People's Army's Soviet-supplied T-34 tanks swiftly dominated the battlefield. The South had no tanks and few effective anti-tank weapons. The outcome was predictable.

Likewise, the US light tanks rushed to South Korea to help were no match for the T-34. Field guns firing over open sights were about all they could use to stop the North's tanks. Once the US Sherman, Pershing and Patton began to arrive the T-34's dominance came to an end. However, there were few full-scale tank battles. Tanks on both sides soon found themselves relegated to their original role of providing infantry support or acting as mobile artillery and pillboxes.

The seeds of the Korean War were sown by the Japanese occupation. From 1910 until 1945 Japan controlled the Korean peninsula. Soviet leader Joseph Stalin cynically invaded Japanese-held Manchuria in the summer of 1945 and the Red Army then rolled south into Korea. After the Japanese surrendered Soviet troops occupied the country north of the 38th parallel, while US forces were deployed to the south. The Koreans themselves had not been consulted about this division, which had been taken by the Allies at Potsdam that summer.

The country became a victim of the developing Cold War in which the West sought to contain the expansion of Communism. In fact, Korea became the scene of the first major armed conflict of the Cold War. Just as Stalin had occupied Eastern Europe it soon became clear that he had no intention of vacating North Korea until the Korean Communists were firmly in power.

The North Koreans soon moved to assist the Chinese Communists who were struggling to defeat the US-backed Chinese Nationalist armies. After the Communist victory in 1949 about 50,000 armed North Korean volunteers were sent home. China also pledged to support the North in the event of a war with the South.

Tension began to mount especially after the North's Communist government refused to hold free elections. Despite vague reunification talks, cross-border skirmishes became a regular occurrence. The Soviet Union finally withdrew in 1948 with the USA following suit the year after. While the Soviets left in place a fairly powerful army, in contrast the South Korean army was poorly equipped and was little more than a police force. Stalin ensured that Korean Communist leader Kim Il-Sung's forces were equipped with hundreds of tanks, artillery, fighters and bombers – weapons that had been tried and tested during the Second World War.

Kim Il-Sung went to Moscow in April 1950 and gained Stalin's support for a unified Korea under his control. Stalin was cautious for although agreeing to reunification by force, he was reluctant to come into open conflict with the West, especially when he was still consolidating his position in Eastern Europe. The following month Kim travelled to Beijing and saw the Chinese Communist leader Chairman Mao Tse-tung.

Again, Mao was cautious about being dragged into a war over Korea. The Communist People's Republic of China had only come into being in October 1949. His country was exhausted by the civil war and he was eyeing Taiwan (where the Chinese Nationalists were holding out) and Tibet. Also, the Chinese People's Liberation Army (PLA) was in the process of demobilising 50 per cent of the 5.6 million men it had under arms. The burden of maintaining this force was just too great.

Communist North Korea invaded the South on 25 June 1950 brushing aside the South's small Army. Dramatically, Seoul fell just two days later. Having watched China fall to the Communists, it now looked as if the West would have to adjust to the shock of seeing a second Asian country submit to Communism within a year.

President Truman was not keen on sacrificing US lives over Korea, especially as the country was not included in the Asian defence perimeter strategy. Besides, the Soviet threat was much more immediate in Europe than in Asia. Nonetheless, the

USA was obliged to address any threat to Japan. If the whole of the Korean peninsula fell under the Communist sway then Japan was clearly in danger. At the same time, Truman was not blind to the danger of Stalin using Korea as a diversion before he attacked Europe.

The United Nations (UN) acted promptly and on 7 July US General Douglas MacArthur was appointed to command UN forces that would be sent to assist South Korea. US forces were brushed aside at Osan and Taejon and the UN and South Korean forces were forced to fight a defensive war. The Battle for the Pusan perimeter began on 1 August 1950 but by 14 September the North Koreans had been beaten off. The following day a US amphibious force landed at Inchon and within a week had retaken Seoul. By the end of the month North Korean resistance in the South had dramatically all but ceased.

The UN then invaded the North, some would say unwisely, provoking Chinese intervention in November and the UN forces were pushed back to the 38th Parallel. The Communists launched their 'First Spring Offensive' on 22 April 1951, though by the end of the month it was spent. The conflict then degenerated into a static war of attrition. By July 1952 both sides were so well dug in that neither could launch a major offensive without considerable casualties. An armistice was finally signed on 27 July 1953 leaving both sides armed camps to this very day.

Photograph Sources

Over 180 contemporary photographs have been selected for this fascinating book to show Soviet-built T-34/85s and SU-76s, US M4 Shermans, M26 Pershings and M46 Pattons, and British Churchills, Cromwells and Centurions in action in one of the defining conflicts of the Cold War years.

The vast majority of images in this book are drawn primarily from US Department of Defense sources and were taken by members of the US Army, Navy, Air Force and Marine Corps. The US National Archives and Records Administration depositories now hold many of the originals. The other much smaller UN military contingents, particularly from Britain and the Commonwealth, also produced a good visual record of the conflict.

Due to the differences in the armies involved, the North Koreans and Chinese forces were chiefly made up of masses of infantry, there is a notable disparity in the types and volume of tanks, armoured vehicles, artillery and fighter jets that were photographed during the Korean War.

Perhaps not surprisingly, the North Koreans and Chinese had little concept of war photography and therefore photographic records on their side of the conflict are largely wanting. What was produced was almost entirely for propaganda purposes. Western photographers on the whole took those photographs of Communist military equipment, particularly the North Korean T-34 tanks. In the opening stages the latter provided a particular source of fascination for Western forces.

The author hopes the reader enjoys the following selection of images that are designed to offer some insight into aspects of a major war that occurred within less than a decade of the Second World War ending.

Chapter One

Uncle Joe's Koreans

At the start of the war the North Korean People's Army (NKPA) had about 223,000 men under arms, with 8 infantry divisions at full strength, 2 more at half-strength, various support regiments and most importantly an armoured brigade. The NKPA was under General Choi Yung Kun who answered to the Supreme Commander, Field Marshal Kim Il-Sung. Relative to other armies in the region, it was well equipped and well trained; the Soviet Union had been overseeing its development since 1945.

Just three months after Nazi Germany surrendered, the Red Army invaded Manchukuo – the Japanese puppet state in Manchuria, and went on to also attack neighbouring Mengjiang, northern Korea, southern Sakhalin and the Kuril Islands. The invasion was conducted between the two atomic bombs dropped on Hiroshima on 6 August and Nagasaki on 9 August 1945.

The fighting lasted less than a week before the Japanese declared a ceasefire. The results were to be far reaching. Soviet-occupied Manchuria provided the main base for Mao's Chinese Communist forces that would eventually seize power in China. The creation of a Communist state in North Korea led to the Korean War.

Japanese and Chinese relations had first come to a head in 1894 when they fought bitterly over Korea. The outcome was the Treaty of Shimonoseki, China abandoned her rights to Korea ceding not only the Laiodong Peninsula in the north, but also Taiwan and the Pescadore Islands.

A decade later Japan turned on Imperial Russia attacking her fleet at Port Arthur, taking over the latter and gaining Russia's rights in the southern part of Manchuria. China acquiesced to this even granting the Japanese further concessions in the cities of Manchuria. In 1915 the Twenty-One Demands saw China cede all Germany's regional rights to Tokyo effectively making China a Japanese protectorate.

The humiliation of Russia's forces in 1904 and 1905 ensured that simmering resentment marred their relations during the 1920s and 1930s. This was aggravated by Japan's seizure of Chinese Manchuria, which became the puppet state of Manchukuo. After the Japanese occupation of Korea and Manchuria friction between Japan and the Soviet Union was inevitable. However, following fighting at

Khalkhin-Gol the Russo-Japanese dispute was settled with a border treaty in June 1940 and twelve months latter Adolf Hitler attacked the Soviet Union.

After the Second World War the NKPA's Soviet-supplied equipment made the neighbouring Chinese PLA look like a rabble. Most of the North's weaponry was Red Army surplus and battle proven courtesy of the generosity of 'Uncle Joe' Stalin – some of it had come via Soviet freighter from Vladivostok as late as May 1950 just before the North invaded the South.

One of the first things the Soviets did was instruct the North Koreans in the technicalities of mechanised warfare; a tank training unit was set up at Sadong, where the crews of the NKPA's armoured battalion took to their massive Soviet T-34/85 tanks with enthusiasm.

The 105th Armoured Battalion established in October 1948 was the NKPA's very first armoured unit. The following May it became a regiment and was then strengthened to become a brigade in June 1950 with 6,000 men equipped with 120 T-34/85s. It consisted of three regiments, the 107th, 109th and 203rd, each with forty tanks, supported by the 206th Mechanised Infantry Regiment; the 308th self-propelled artillery regiment equipped with sixteen SU-76 self-propelled guns provided artillery firepower.

Similarly, the North Koreans were given plenty of artillery, each division was equipped with 12 heavy 122mm howitzers, plus 24 lighter 76.2mm field guns, 12 SU-76 self-propelled guns and 12 45mm anti-tank guns. The infantry was issued with its own supporting 120mm and 82mm heavy mortars. Small arms consisted of the Soviet PPsh41 submachine gun and SKS carbine. They had a ready supply of radios, medicines and trucks. In addition, the Soviets provided the NKPA with about 180 new aircraft, 40 of which were Yakovlev fighters and another 70 were attack bombers.

The men who formed the backbone of the NKPA were drawn from the 16,000 repatriated Korean veterans who fought in the Chinese Civil War. Just two months before the NKPA attacked the South the Chinese PLA transferred at Pyongyang's request an additional 12,000 veterans. In April 1947 about 30,000 Koreans under General Kim Chaek had moved into Manchuria and by May up to 20 per cent of the Chinese Communist forces in Manchuria were Koreans. Rather confusingly, US intelligence dubbed them Chinese Communist forces or CCF Koreans; this made it initially hard to identify ethnic Chinese troops when they actually entered the war.

Intelligence reports indicated that the Chinese 4th Army under veteran Lin Bao numbered 145,000 Koreans. This field army was a crack force that had never lost a battle against the Chinese Nationalists as it rolled southwards into Manchuria. The Nationalists estimated that there were 50,000 Koreans with Chinese Communist forces south of the Great Wall, so the number of Koreans who had seen military action in China was probably about the 100,000 mark.

Although these men were combat hardened, they were not trained in Soviet-style mechanised warfare – the majority had never even seen a tank before. The veterans released to the NKPA helped flesh out the 1st, 4th, 5th 6th and 7th Divisions. In addition, the North had a 19,000-strong border force raised from Koreans who had lived in the Soviet Union. 'Uncle Joe's' Koreans were ready for battle.

Very confident-looking Japanese officers about to board a flight. The seeds of the Korean War were sown in 1894 when the Imperial Japanese Army occupied Korea. It was then used as a springboard to attack China and carve out a puppet state in Manchuria bordering the Soviet Union. (*Author's Collection*)

More Japanese officers somewhere in Manchuria. The Japanese presence there sparked fighting with the Soviet Union at Khalkhin-Gol in 1939. While the peace treaty that followed enabled Stalin to concentrate on defeating Hitler, it meant he had unfinished business with the Japanese. (*Author's Collection*)

A rather blurred shot of Red Army tank crews posing with a T-34/85 tank and a SU-100 assault gun somewhere in the Soviet Far East. Stalin gifted the fledgling NKPA almost 300 armoured fighting vehicles. T-34 tanks were handed over to the North Koreans to create the 105th Armoured Battalion which was later increased to brigade strength. (*Author's Collection*)

At the end of the Second World War Stalin attacked Japanese-held Manchuria and the Red Army then rolled south into Korea occupying the country north of the 38th Parallel. The Japanese had no way of fending off the powerful T-34/85 tank seen here. (*Author's Collection*)

Dividing Korea along the 38th Parallel positioned the Red Army in the North and the US Army in the South. When they withdrew the country was supposed to be reunited following elections but this did not happen. (*US DoD*)

(*Opposite, top*) US General Douglas MacArthur had responsibility for the US forces stationed in Japan and South Korea at the end of the Second World War. A conflict in Korea was the last thing he wanted. (*US DoD*)

(*Opposite, below*) A row of T-34/85 tanks. Stalin provided the North Koreans with 120 of these, which in June 1950 formed the 105th Armoured Brigade consisting of 3 tank regiments. A further 30 were issued to a tank training unit. (*Chris Streckfus*)

US forces in the Far East were not anticipating having to fight a major conventional war just five years after the end of the Second World War. (*US DoD*)

Another armoured fighting vehicle supplied to the North Koreans, this time the SU-76 assault gun, while just behind it is a 76.2mm field gun. Like the T-34, these weapons were veterans of the Second World War and the Soviets had them in abundance. (*Via Author*)

As well as tanks and self-propelled guns, the North Koreans were given plenty of Soviet artillery that included 122mm and 76.2mm (seen here) guns. (*Via Author*)

The NKPA infantry divisions' self-propelled gun battalions fielded a total of 120 SU-76. A self-propelled gun battalion was also assigned to the 105th Armoured Brigade. The open fighting compartment left the crews exposed to shellfire. (*Via Author*)

US forces examining a captured North Korean Yakovlev fighter at Kimpo Air Field, west of Seoul following the Inchon landings. In the run-up to the war the Soviets provided the NKPA with 180 aircraft, of which 40 were Yaks. (*US DoD*)

This photograph illustrates the contrasts in the landscape of the Korean peninsula. These fur-capped South Korean Army officers are manning an observation post overlooking the disputed border in late June 1950. (*US DoD*)

Again this photograph shows that Korea was not ideal tank country. The wires belong to the overhead tramway of the 97th Infantry Regiment, US 40th Infantry Division in July 1952. (*US DoD*)

The landscape often favoured the defenders. These members of the US 27th Infantry Regiment are dug in on a hill top firing on exposed North Korean positions on 4 September 1950. (*US DoD*)

Chapter Two

The North Korean Steamroller

For the invasion of South Korea seven NKPA divisions were gathered under General Kim Chaek and grouped into the 1st Army, consisting of the 1st, 3rd, 4th and 6th Divisions as well as the 105th Armoured Brigade, and the weaker 2nd Army with the 2nd, 5th and 7th Divisions. The 1st Army was given the job of overrunning the Ongjin Peninsula and the South Korean capital Seoul.

It was the NKPA's tanks that provided the key striking force. 'The enemy, after penetrating the defences with his armour,' General Matthew B. Ridgway, who commanded the US 8th Army in Korea, noted, 'would envelop both flanks with infantry, surround artillery units, and roll on rearward.'

Crucially, the NKPA opened the war with about 150 T-34/85 tanks armed with the 85mm gun, which was superior to anything else in theatre at the time. The UN forces were to dub them 'Caviar Cans'. While 120 tanks were deployed with the 105th Armoured Brigade, the NKPA infantry divisions' self-propelled gun battalions fielded a total of 120 Soviet-supplied SU-76 assault guns. In addition to the tanks of the armoured brigade, the personnel from the tank training unit at Sadong with a further thirty tanks were assigned to the 7th Division. They deployed on the east-central front for the attack on Inje.

In the early stages of the fighting the North Koreans also used their tanks in built-up areas with some considerable effect neutralising UN defenders. During the assault on Taejon they moved in pairs or singularly carrying supporting infantry. Afterwards, though, they used their armour much more circumspectly because of improving US counter-measures.

After the capture of the South Korean capital the 105th Armoured Brigade became the 105th 'Seoul' Armoured Division and was strengthened with the 308th Self-propelled Battalion. The 3rd and 4th Divisions which were also involved were likewise given the honorary title 'Seoul Division'. By 1953 the NKPA had seven tank regiments (104–107th, 109th, 206th and 208th).

During the battles for the Pusan pocket the NKPA received reinforcements including another eighty T-34/85, which equipped two new tank units, the 16th and 17th Armoured Brigades. Some were also sent to the 105th Armoured Brigade, but the UN's air supremacy meant that many were destroyed before they could reach the front. UN estimates at the end of September 1950 were that the entire NKPA T-34 force (then believed to stand at 239) had been destroyed whereas UN forces had only lost 60 tanks.

While the Chinese Nationalist forces had created a mechanised division, equipped initially with Soviet and then US-supplied tanks, the Communists had never taken to armour and simply relied on manpower alone. Soviet assistance to the Nationalists stopped once Moscow had signed a non-aggression pact with Tokyo. The PLA produced a copy of the Soviet T-34/85 in the 1950s known as the Type 58, but few if any saw combat in Korea. It is likely that most of the Soviet T-34s supplied to the PLA were passed on to the NKPA.

Reports of Chinese tanks in Korea are non-existent. Although on 26 October 1950 when the Republic of Korea's (RoK) Army's 26th Division came up against the Chinese 124th Division, General Matthew B. Ridgway reported, 'When the Marines came up to relieve the RoKs a few days later they met and destroyed Chinese tanks (the only ones the X Corps was to encounter) and picked up prisoners from a fresh Chinese division, the 126th.' One can only assume that Ridgway was mistaken and these were supporting NKPA tanks, though it is always possible the Chinese brought a few with them.

China committed six armies each of three divisions in support of the NKPA in November 1950. Significantly, they had no tanks, vehicles or artillery, allowing these units to slip into North Korea largely undetected. The Chinese armies also lacked air support. To compensate for the lack of anti-tank weapons each platoon was issued with 2.25kg TNT satchel charges sufficient to take the track off a tank. It was not until the summer of 1951 that the Chinese began to deploy artillery and mortars.

In north-western Korea the PLA assembled the Chinese 9th Army Group under General Song Shilun. This was a new command consisting of 120,000 men who were tasked with taking on the US Marines around the Changjin Reservoir. Two of Shilun's three field armies, the 20th and 26th, had been detached from the forces once earmarked to attack the Nationalist-held island of Taiwan; the 27th Field Army came from Shandong and each of the three were supplemented by one division from the 30th Field Army.

Facing the US 8th Army was the PLA's 13th Army Group totalling 180,000 men and commanded by Lieutenant Li Tianyu. His forces initially saw action at Unsan, along the Chongchon River and in the area of the Changjin Reservoir. Tianyu's original three field armies, the 38th, 40th and 42nd, were rapidly reinforced with the 39th, 50th and 66th Field armies.

Notably, the 50th Field Army consisted of former Nationalist troops who had surrendered in Manchuria in 1948. Their commander, Lieutenant General Zeng Zesheng, had spent most of his career fighting the Communists. Three years earlier he had worked with David Barr, the US advisor to the Nationalist forces, who now commanded the US 7th Infantry Division fighting on the other side. Zesheng's former Nationalist Corps were almost wiped out in the final battle for Seoul.

As well as armour, artillery and fighter aircraft the PLA lacked even the most rudimentary logistical support. Soldiers were expected to carry what food and ammunition they needed to fight. Only 800 trucks belonging to the 5th and 42nd Truck Regiments were assigned to support the troops in Korea. Only 50 per cent were expected to remain operational. In addition, over ½ million coolies were recruited to carry supplies across the Yalu River, but they created their own logistical headache, as they had to be fed and housed over considerable distances. Many Chinese commanders considered them an unwanted distraction and a drain on resources.

North Korea came about thanks to the support of Soviet leader Joseph Stalin and Chinese Communist Mao Tse-tung for Korean communist leader Kim Il-Sung. These pictures were found in the city of Wonsan. (*US DoD*)

The NKPA's T-34 tanks provided its key striking force. Initially, the South Korean and US armies had no answer to these well-armoured monsters. This tank was brought to a stop in the Waegwan area in South Korea after a fighter from the US 5th Air Force destroyed the wooden bridge it was crossing. Note how the welds on the front of the hull have been ripped open by the force of the blast. (*US DoD*)

More NKPA T-34s knocked out – these two were caught on the road. The UN forces dubbed them 'Caviar Cans'. On the whole, North Korean tanks had free rein until they had forced the South Korean and US armies back into the Pusan perimeter. (*US DoD*)

US Marines guarding three captured North Korean infantry, who have been stripped to ensure they are not concealing any weapons or explosives. The NKPA started the war with 223,000 men under arms, many of whom had previously fought alongside the Chinese Communists. (*US DoD*)

US troops from the 389th Infantry Regiment interrogating two incredibly young North Korean recruits captured on 18 September 1950 in the Sindang-dong area. (*US DoD*)

Once US air power came into play there was no hiding for the North Koreans' tanks. Rather incongruously this T-34 remained intact but trapped after the USAF destroyed the concrete bridge it was crossing south of Suwon on 7 October 1950. The open turret hatches either indicate the crew fled or the vehicle was later examined by local US forces. (*US DoD*)

Hiding under a bridge near the Naktong River did this North Korean T-34 no good. US fighter bombers or artillery simply brought the span down on top of it. The photo also shows US engineers constructing a Bailey bridge replacement in late September 1950. (*US DoD*)

With the UN forces pushing the NKPA back toward the Chinese border, the PLA was committed to the war in the winter of 1950. These Chinese soldiers in warm quilted uniforms were captured by the US 1st Marine Division in the spring of 1951. The PLA relied on manpower alone, and Chinese tanks were conspicuous by their absence. (*US DoD*)

(*Opposite*) Another NKPA PoW taken during the Naktong River engagements on 4 September 1950. He is sitting on a US Military Police jeep. Many NKPA recruits were veterans of the Chinese Civil War. (*US DoD*)

The crew of a 75mm recoilless rifle from the US 1st Regimental Combat Team engaging enemy targets near Oetlook-tong on 9 June 1951. This weapon first shipped over from Japan with Task Force Smith and along with the unit's 2.36in bazookas were incapable of knocking out the T-34. (*US DoD*)

(*Opposite, top*) US troops putting down a barrage on the Yongdock area with 105mm howitzers on 23 July 1950; note the spent shell cases in the foreground. It was superior US firepower in the shape of artillery and then tanks and fighter bombers that held the North Koreans at bay once the Pusan perimeter was created. (*US DoD*)

(*Opposite, below*) US Marines displaying a North Korean flag during the push on the Chosin Reservoir. The troops of the NKPA proved to be tough adversaries. (*US DoD*)

Once it became apparent that the Chinese had openly sided with North Korea it was imperative that the bridges over the Yalu River dividing the two be cut. This dramatic photograph shows a US bomber recovering from a dive after dropping a 2,000lb bomb on the Korean side of a bridge over the Yalu at Sinuiju. Judging by all the craters the area had already taken a heavy pounding. (*US DoD*)

Chapter Three

RoK's Armour

During the Japanese occupation many Koreans were conscripted into the Imperial Japanese Army, while others fought for the Soviets and the Chinese. After the Japanese military surrendered to the USA south of the 38th Parallel former Japanese Army veterans were used to form a 15,000-strong Korean Constabulary. In 1948 they became the South's army, which was expanded to 60,000 to counter North Korean border raids and internal subversion.

Disastrously, South Korea, or more correctly the Republic of Korea (RoK), at the start of the Korean War had no tanks or effective anti-tank weapons. Due to the RoK's inadequate defences the NKPA's armour understandably had a demoralising effect on its troops. When North Korea invaded the NKPA's tanks just simply drove down the roads in column. They sliced straight through the South Korean positions, while the NKPA's infantry surrounded them and finished the job.

To be fair the South Korean security forces had little need for tanks as their main role was countering ill-equipped Communist insurgents who caused a headache for the authorities throughout the late 1940s. On the large Korean island of Cheju, which lies to the south-west of the Korean peninsula, much of the interior was taken over by the 4,000-strong People's Army. The fighting that followed to stamp them out resulted in around 20,000 islanders being killed.

There were 2 RoK regiments, numbering 2,000 troops, destined for Cheju and these rebelled in the southern port city of Yosu. Although this rebellion had been put down by late 1948, the mainland suffered from organised guerrilla warfare being conducted by up to 6,000 fighters. It was believed that the hand of North Korea was behind all this unrest, though there was little evidence of Soviet or North Korean support for the southern guerrillas. Most of them had Japanese or US weapons, though some Soviet ones were found near the 38th Parallel.

Before leaving, the US military had trained the RoK Army. However, it was little more than a paramilitary police force and in June 1950 only numbered about 98,000 men. Just three of its seven infantry divisions were up to full strength and these were guarding the 38th Parallel (the dividing line between the North and

South). The only armour RoK possessed were twenty-seven M8 armoured cars belonging to the Capital Division in Seoul.

Major General Chae Pyongdok's forces had no medium artillery, heavy mortars, air support or armour, except for the armoured car cavalry regiment with the Capital Division. His men were equipped with just rifles, carbines, light mortars and 2.36in bazookas (which were ineffective against the T-34 tank) and 140 light 37mm anti-tank guns. The entire RoK Army only had 91 US-supplied M3 105mm howitzers organised into three artillery battalions supporting the 7th and 8th Divisions and the elite 17th Independent Regiment. Under US organisation there should have been 432 divisional artillery pieces supported by other independent artillery battalions. This lack of firepower was to cost the RoK Army dearly.

Of RoK's eight divisions only the 1st, 6th, 7th infantry and Capitol Divisions were at full strength, fielding about 11,000 men each; they along with the 8th Division were the best units. However, the 6th Division was one of the few units that was actually combat ready before the invasion having just undergone a bout of intensive training. The outcome of any initial clash between the RoK Army and the heavily armed NKPA when it invaded was inevitable.

Although the soldiers of the RoK fought hard there was little they could do against the North's heavy weaponry. Both the 6th and the 1st Divisions made gallant efforts to try and stem the tide of NKPA troops. After the fall of Seoul the 1st, 2nd, 3rd, 5th, 7th and Capitol Divisions retreated south, while the 6th and 8th headed east. Almost half the army, some 44,000 men, were trapped north of the Han River after the bridges were blown too early.

After fighting at Taejon alongside the USA the RoK Army withdrew into the 160-mile Pusan perimeter. The remains of 5 RoK divisions numbering 45,000 men defended the northern side, while 30,000 troops of the US 1st Cavalry and 24th Infantry Divisions defended the western side. During the summer the US 2nd Infantry Division, 1st Provincial Marine Brigade and the British 27th Infantry Brigade arrived as reinforcements.

Inside the Pusan perimeter RoK's 8th and Capitol Divisions formed I Corps; 1st and 6th the II Corps and the 3rd was assigned to Army Headquarters. The rest were disbanded. The III Corps was formed in October for security duties comprising the 5th and newly formed 11th Divisions.

Following the Inchon landings by late November 1950 the Capitol Division was within 60 miles of the Soviet border. The Chinese though were able to take advantage of the poor firepower of the RoK divisions. Once they had forced the US 8th Army to withdraw the exposed Capitol and 3rd Divisions fell back on Songjin and Hungnam respectively and had to be evacuated to South Korea. The US Navy successfully rescued 105,000 troops, 91,000 Korean refugees, 17,000 vehicles and several hundred tons of supplies from Hungnam.

It was not until April 1951 that a South Korean armoured force was finally formed as part of the infantry school near Kwangju. This was equipped with US M24 Chaffee light tanks and M36B2 tank destroyers. It first went into action in October 1951 on the east-central front. By mid-1952 the RoK Army had eight tank companies (51st–53rd and 55th–59th) giving it far greater punch. Nonetheless, the vast bulk of tanks deployed in Korea belonged to the US armed forces.

At the start of the war the South Korean Army's armour consisted of two-dozen US M8 armoured cars. It was not until the spring of 1951 that the South Koreans created an armoured force equipped with US-supplied M24 Chaffee light tanks, seen here, and M36B2 Tank Destroyers. (*Author's Collection*)

An M24 light tank in action somewhere in Korea during the summer of 1951. The Chaffee was another veteran of the Second World War and although it had not entered service until late 1944 armed with a 75mm gun, it packed quite a punch for its small size. (*US DoD*)

(*Opposite, top*) When the North invaded the South Korean Army had 140 US 37mm anti-tank guns that were completely incapable of dealing with the T-34. The RoK Army numbered less that 100,000 so were outnumbered 2 : 1. (*US DoD*)

(*Opposite, below*) The South Koreans also had the M1A1 2.36in rocket launcher, better known as the bazooka, which was even more ineffective against the NKPA's T-34s. This weapon was replaced by the 3.4in rocket launcher, seen here, that enjoyed much greater success. The North Koreans lost twenty tanks to this weapon during their attack on Taejon on 20 July 1950. (*US DoD*)

Initially, the RoK Army had less than 100 M2A1 105mm howitzers; enough to support just 2 infantry divisions. These particular guns belong to the US Army. (*US DoD*)

(*Opposite, top*) As the war progressed the South's 105mm artillery was upgraded. Here South Korean gunners of the 88th Field Artillery are firing a 155mm howitzer at Chinese Communist positions during fighting for the Shanghai Heights area, west of Chorwon at the end of October 1952. (*US DoD*)

(*Opposite, below*) General MacArthur inspecting troops in Korea. He was not happy at the state of the RoK Army or indeed US forces in Japan, and their weakness undoubtedly encouraged North Korea to invade. (*US DoD*)

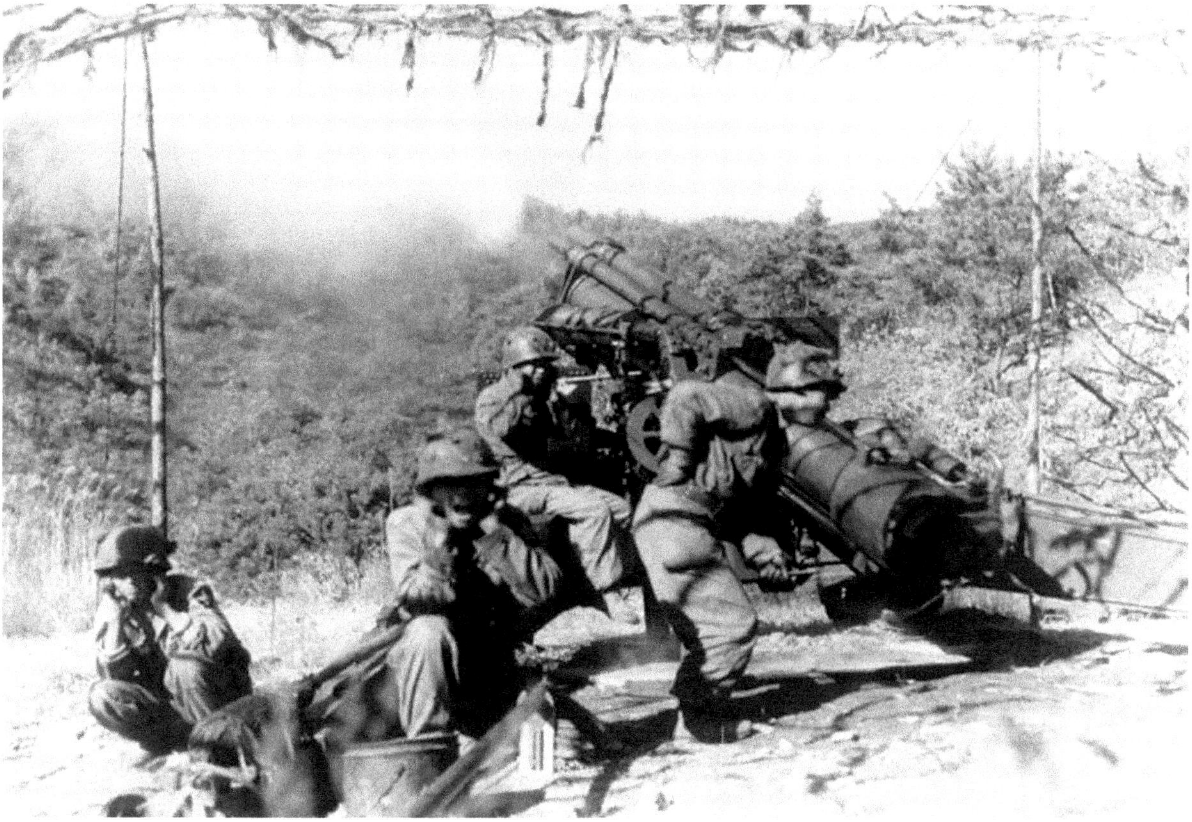

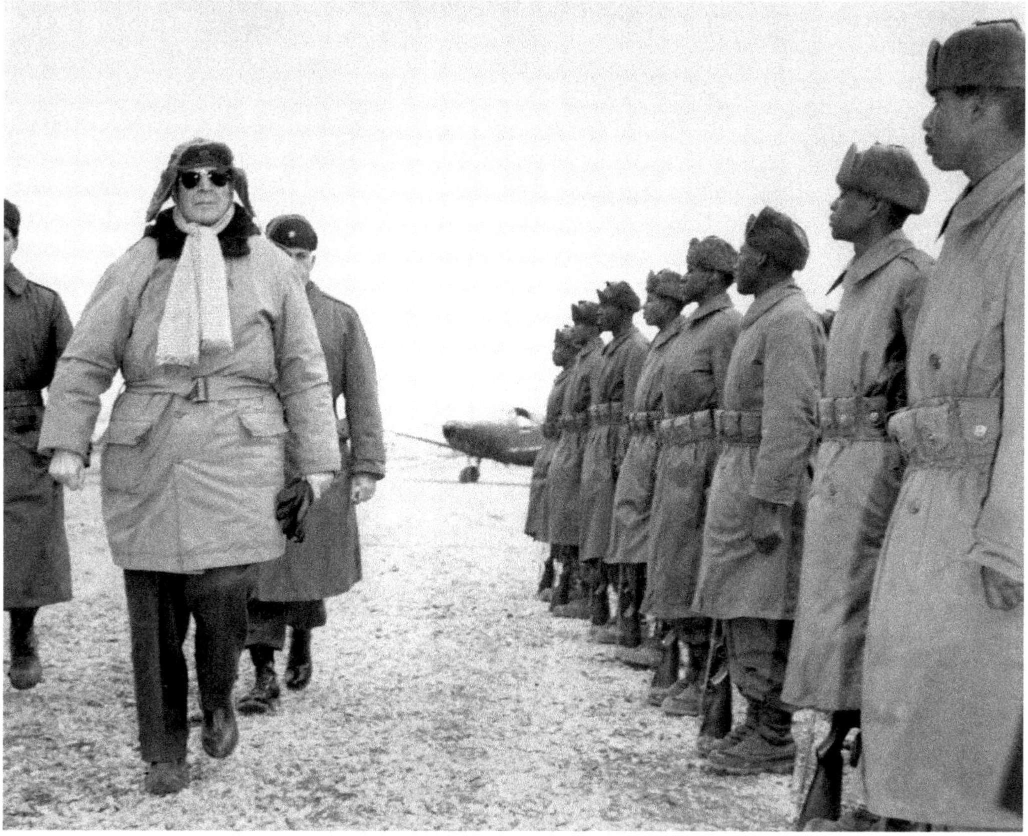

The USA initially only had three M26 Pershing medium tanks armed with a powerful 90mm gun in Korea; these were soon reinforced by more M26s and the improved version known as the M46 Patton (identifiable by the small additional rear road wheel). Although the Pershing was the most powerful US tank of the Second World War, it only joined the US armoured divisions in the closing months of the conflict and saw very little combat. (*US DoD*)

At the start of the Korean War the USA was reliant on M4A3 Sherman HVSS (the Horizontal Volute Spring Suspension armed with a 76mm gun) with the 89th Tank Battalion – this tank was yet another Second World War veteran. (*Author's Collection*)

In the face of invasion by the North, the USA rushed US Army and Marine reinforcements to South Korea. It was almost too little too late as the remains of the RoK Army were trapped in the Pusan perimeter and almost overwhelmed. (*US DoD*)

A line of US jeeps queuing for the ferry across the Kumho-gang River in mid-September 1950. The muddy road gives some indication of the poor condition of Korea's highways. (*US DoD*)

US engineers check a road for mines in the path of a US Sherman tank – fifty-four such tanks had to be hurriedly rebuilt in Japan and rushed to Korea in late July 1950. At the time the USA only had a single armoured division. (*US DoD*)

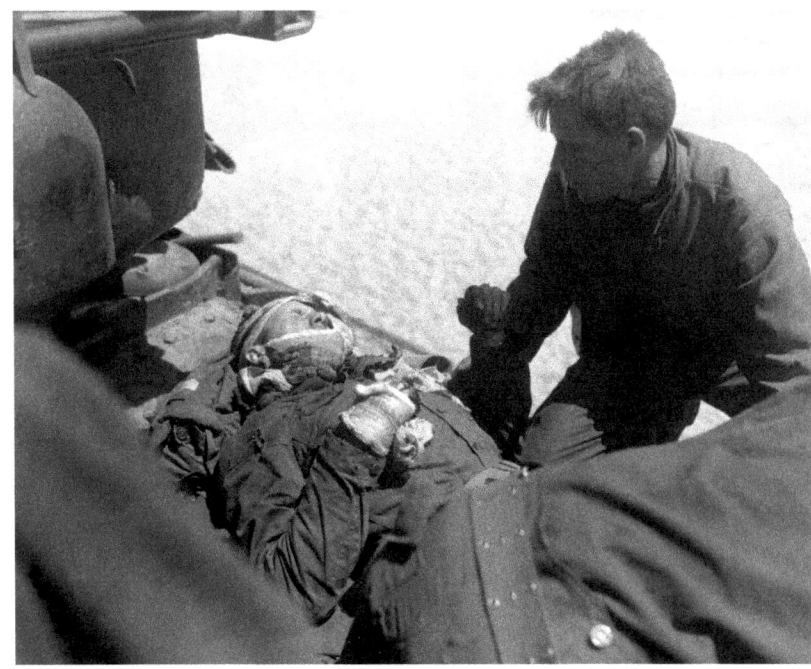

A casualty is treated on the back of a tank belonging to the US 89th Tank Battalion during the fighting north-east of Seoul. This unit along with the 77th Tank Battalion were the only ones available to help in the early stages of the invasion. (*US DoD*)

A US 105mm howitzer of the 159th Field Artillery Battalion provides indirect fire support for the South Korean Army near Uirson on 24 August 1950. The elevation of the gun shows they are firing at maximum range; only the rapid build-up of US armour, artillery and fighter bombers saved the South from being completely overrun following its stand at Pusan. (*US DoD*)

US infantry take cover from incoming fire. On 1 July 1950 Task Force Smith from the US 24th Division was rushed to the front, consisting of 2 rifle companies numbering just 500 lightly armed men. (*US DoD*)

In the face of the rapid advance by the NKPA and then the PLA
trapped RoK Army units often had to be evacuated by sea. (*US DoD*)

Chapter Four

Uncle Sam Holds the Line

In the wake of the Second World War much of the US Army was demobilised and sent home. At the outbreak of the Korean War it only had ten combat divisions including a single armoured division. The US presence in South Korea consisted of a mere 500 advisors who were busy training the RoK Army and advising on counter-insurgency operations. Although never deployed in large numbers, US armour was to be instrumental in providing fire support and static defence.

General Douglas MacArthur's US forces stationed in nearby Japan were only equipped with M24 Chaffee light tanks as it was feared anything heavier would damage Japanese roads and bridges. In the face of invasion Lieutenant General Walton H. Walker's 8th Army, which was on occupation duties in Japan, was put on alert. Four light tank battalions supported his infantry divisions; the 71st, 77th, 78th and 79th but each of these were only of company strength.

In response to the T-34 tank's success in Korea the 8072nd Medium Tank Battalion (later re-designated the 89th) was quickly activated in Japan with fifty-four rebuilt M4A3 Sherman HVSS armed with a 76mm anti-tank gun. The USA quickly rushed this armour over to support their forces in South Korea in late July 1950.

In the meantime, Task Force Smith from the US 24th Infantry Division was hurried to the front on 1 July 1950 and held up the NKPA's advance on Osan. This numbered just 500 men, consisting of 2 rifle companies, 2 platoons of 4.2in mortars, a single 75mm recoilless rifle crew and 6 2.36in bazooka teams. None of these weapons were capable of knocking out the NKPA's T-34s. For several days they were the only US fighting force on the ground and had to contend with massed enemy troops, tanks and artillery.

On 5 July 1950 the NKPA's armour first came up against the USA. Some thirty-three T-34/85s of the 107th Armoured Regiment took part in the attack. Advancing in groups of four T-34/85s with all guns blazing, the Americans were only able to stop two tanks using high-explosive anti-tank (HEAT) rounds. Only four were immobilised and after seven hours of fighting the USA was forced to withdraw with its tail between its legs.

'At 8am on 5 July, the enemy attacked near Osan with 30 tanks and a strong force of infantry,' General Ridgway later wrote. 'Task Force Smith soon had to choose between retreat and annihilation. Having held their positions until their ammunition was gone, they withdrew in some disorder, receiving heavy casualties.' At Taejon the 24th Infantry Division gained valuable time for the arrival of the 25th Infantry and 1st Cavalry Divisions from Japan as well as the 29th Regimental Combat Team from Okinawa.

Five days later three of the completely inadequate US M24 light tanks came up against the T-34/85 at Chonui for the first time. They fared little better and lost two tanks, though they did manage to destroy a single T-34. The US government put three tank battalions on alert in the USA on 10 July 1950, the 6th with the M46 Patton belonging to the 2nd Armoured Division, 70th with the M26 Pershing and M4A3 Sherman and 73rd also with the M26 Pershing; the latter two were school troop battalions from the Armour School at Fort Knox and Infantry School at Fort Benning. They were the only armoured units in the USA combat ready and they arrived at Pusan on 7 August 1950.

It was not until late July 1950 that an effective infantry anti-tank weapon was supplied in the shape of the 3.5in rocket launcher known as the bazooka. The NKPA's attack on the city of Taejon on 20 July saw ten tanks lost to this weapon the very first time it was deployed. However, in one case it took three rockets before the crew was killed and the tank immobilised. The victor was none other than Major General William F. Dean, commander of the 24th Infantry Division who was to later boast 'I got me a tank!'

Three refurbished M26 Pershings (the only medium tanks in the whole of Korea) crewed by men from the 77th Tank Battalion engaged the enemy at Chinju on 31 July. A blown-up bridge cut off their retreat and they had to be abandoned – another humiliation for the USA. On 2 August the newly arrived M4A3 HVSS went into action for the first time with better results.

With the loss of Taejon the UN forces fell back to the Pusan perimeter. There US Marine M26s were used in a defensive role and in the battle of the Naktong Bulge, in which the 1st Marine Provisional Brigade under the 24th Infantry Division tried to destroy the NKPA 4th Division bridgehead over the river. The tide was about to turn against the T-34.

On 12 July Company 'A', 1st Marine Tank Battalion, which was used to the M4A3 but reissued with the Pershing, as well as units of the 1st Marine Amphibian Tractor Battalion sailed from the USA. The were committed first to the Sachon counteroffensive, then during the fighting between Observation Hill and Hill 125 a Pershing came face to face with a T-34 from the 107th Armoured Regiment. This and a second T-34 were knocked out by a combination of the Pershing's 90mm gun and bazooka and recoilless rifle fire.

By the end of August the USA had over 500 medium tanks in Korea, including the M4A3 Sherman, M26 Pershing and M46 Patton. Over 400 of these were in the Pusan pocket, outnumbering the enemy by a least 4 : 1. Although the NKPA received about 100 T-34 replacements, many of them were knocked out by air strikes before they could even reach the battlefield.

The North Koreans were in a race against time in trying to unify the two Koreas and anticipated completing this in about two weeks. Once the Pusan perimeter was formed they soon found themselves heavily outnumbered. By the time of the Inchon landings there were about 83,000 US troops and another 57,000 Korean and British soldiers facing the NKPA. Although North Korea raised the number of its forces along the front to 98,000, over a third of them were raw recruits. This meant that they were unable to withstand the two-pronged attack on Inchon and from Pusan when it came.

A US heavy machine-gun crew engaging Communist forces. At first infantry from the US 24th Infantry Division were on their own in the face of the NKPA's T-34s and SU-76s until Sherman and Pershing tanks could be shipped over from Japan. (*US DoD*)

This NKPA T-34 was one of ten knocked out at Taejon by Major General William F. Dean's US 24th Infantry Division. He later boasted, 'I got me a tank!' He and his men used the 3.5in bazooka to stop them. His resistance at Taejon gained valuable time while two more US divisions were brought over from Japan. (*US DoD*)

This M4A3 (76mm) HVSS Sherman has come a cropper after losing a track to a mine; men from the US 10th Engineer Battalion are examining the tank for Communist booby traps and checking the area for further mines. If the tank could not be recovered it would be blown up to prevent it falling into enemy hands. (*US DoD*)

(*Opposite*) Another Sherman sporting a rather fearsome motif. In early 1951 US armoured fighting vehicles were painted with tiger and dragon designs. This was not on the artistic whim of the crew, but a tactic concocted by the psychological boffins to terrorise Communist forces during the Chinese lunar New Year. One platoon commander of the 89th Tank Battalion said, 'It puts us in running with the Air Force boys with their painted plane noses!' (*US DoD*)

Men from the US 9th Infantry Regiment hitch a ride on a Pershing ready to fight off a Communist attempt to cross the Naktong River on 3 September 1950. Note the spare track links and crew kit hung from the turret. (*US DoD*)

(*Opposite*) A trainload of M46 Pattons heading for the front. Essentially, these were improved versions of the Pershing. These belong to the 1st Tank Battalion, 1st Provisional Marine Brigade which sailed from the USA on 12 July 1950. (*US DoD*)

Another Marine Corps tank about to be shipped to the Far East. The distinctive double barrels identify this as an M4A3 HVSS POA-CWS-H5 Flamethrower of the 1st Marine Tank Battalion. The main barrel is a 105mm gun, while mounted in the mantlet beside it the flamethrower had an effective range of 100yd capable of about eighty 1-second bursts. Such flamethrowers were organised in Flame Sections within HQ and Service Companies of the Marine Tank Battalions. (*US DoD*)

US forces, including a naval commander, examine a Soviet-built North Korean SU-76 self-propelled gun, This 1943–4 vintage armoured fighting vehicle had a 76.2mm gun and a crew of four. The hole on the left in the bow glacis plate may have been what knocked it out. Other battle damage to the mantlet above the gun barrel is just visible. (US DoD)

Another Sherman named 'June', this time from the 32nd Regimental Combat Team, US 7th Infantry Division, disabled by a mine on 28 February 1951. The men are probing the ground for further mines; anti-tank mines were often surrounded by anti-personnel mines to catch escaping crews or the unwary. (US DoD)

Pershing tanks in the harsh winter of 1950–1 keeping a watchful eye on enemy prisoners, although even their mighty firepower was not enough to keep the enormous Chinese Army at bay. (*US DoD*)

Men of Battery B, 15th Anti-Aircraft Artillery Automatic Weapons Battalion (SP), US 7th Infantry Division, fire their quad .50 calibre machine guns mounted in the M16 multiple gun motor carriage at Chinese-held positions in March 1951. This devastating weapon was known appropriately as 'the grinder', 'meat chopper' or more commonly as 'quad-fifty'. (*US DoD*)

The US M39 armored utility vehicle was deployed extensively throughout the Korean War, being used as a personnel carrier and in a medical evacuation, as seen here, and re-supply role. The vehicle was also capable of acting as a mobile mounting for the M55 quad .50 and the 81mm mortar. (*US DoD*)

Another M39 being used to move wounded from the 31st Regiment, US 7th Infantry Division in mid-October 1952. (*US DoD*)

US gunners firing a 105mm howitzer somewhere in Korea. This weapon proved to be a reliable workhorse during the Korean War as it had during the Second World War. (*Author's Collection*)

Known as the 'Gorilla' during the Second World War, the M41 155mm howitzer was based on the chassis of the M24 Chaffee and provided a self-propelled gun with considerable punch. (*US DoD*)

A US machine-gun team formed by Military Police from 10th Corps tries to relieve a convoy pinned down by Chinese troops on 6 December 1950. The Chinese proved very adept at infiltration tactics which enabled them to get in among UN tanks and AFVs so they could attack them at close quarters. (*US DoD*)

This M4 artillery tractor belongs to the 17th Field Artillery, supporting the US 1st Marine Division, in the Chunchon area. Over 5,500 of these vehicles were built during 1943–5 and they were designed to tow 90–240mm artillery. (*US DoD*)

A D-7 bulldozer of the 11th Engineers Battalion, 36th Engineer Group. Such vehicles were vital in keeping Korea's rudimentary roads open. (*US DoD*)

Chapter Five

Britain and the UN to the Rescue

During August other UN forces began to arrive including the 27th British Commonwealth Infantry Brigade, which was later joined by the 29th Infantry Brigade. The 29th Brigade as well as three infantry battalions included tank, artillery and engineer units. The 8th King's Royal Irish Hussars, 1st, 5th and 7th Royal Tank Regiments and 5th Royal Inniskilling Dragoon Guards at various times served with the brigade, while the A, B and C Squadrons Lord Strathcona's Horse deployed with the 25th Canadian Infantry Brigade.

British forces were equipped with Churchill Mk VII infantry support tanks, Cromwell Mk VII cruiser tanks (both veterans of the Second World War) and Centurion Mk 3 main battle tanks. The Canadians initially deployed with M10 self-propelled tank destroyers, then M4A3E8 Shermans.

Churchill Mk VII tanks of C Squadron 7th Royal Tank Regiment were the first British tanks to arrive in Korea. Originally, they were configured as Crocodile flamethrowers, but their trailers were discarded and they were used as standard gun-tanks despite being terribly slow. About 800 Crocodiles were completed by the end of the war. They saw service throughout 1944–5 equipping a tank brigade in North West Europe and were also used in small numbers in Italy.

Along with British Churchills, the Cromwell tanks of 'Cooperforce' fought a rearguard action at Chunghung Dong to cover the withdrawal of 29th Brigade to Seoul. The British Centurion Mk 3 main battle tank was the heaviest tank of the war sporting the thickest armour. Although the slowest, it had a creditable power to weight ratio and better range than the US tanks. Unfortunately, it was never used in great numbers.

The Dingo Mk II Scout Car was used by British Forces in Korea, including the 8th Kings Royal Irish Hussars seeing action on the Imjin River. Most Commonwealth forces in Korea used some variant of the Universal or 'Bren Gun' Carrier (such as the Canadian version the Ford Windsor, the Ford Carrier, Universal No. 3 Mk II and the US T16 Carrier). However, for load carrying they were only suitable for use on roads. The later Oxford Carrier was more successful cross-country but they were not deployed in any great numbers.

When Lord Strathcona's Horse (Royal Canadians) (2nd Armoured Regiment) arrived as part of the 25th Canadian Infantry Brigade they were initially equipped with M10 17-pounder self-propelled Achilles tank destroyers. However, these were exchanged for US M4A3E8 Shermans (prototype for M4A3 76mm HVSS).

When the Korean War broke out the 8th Hussars under Lieutenant Colonel William Lowther BE (Bart) converted to the Centurion Mk 3. They then sailed from Southampton as part of the British 29th Independent Brigade and arrived at Pusan on 14 November 1950. After reaching the front north of Pyongyang they were pushed back to the Han River. Early the following year they lost twenty-three killed or missing during fighting in the 'Compo Valley'.

Captain Donal Astley-Cooper, commanding the Recce troop, put together 'Cooperforce' with Cromwell tanks borrowed from the 7th Battalion, Royal Tank Regiment, which went to the assistance of the Royal Ulster Rifles. The Hussars found themselves caught up in the Battle of Imjin River. Unfortunately, A and B Squadrons had sailed to Japan, leaving C Squadron, initially commanded by Captain Ormrod and then by Major Henry Huth, to hold the Hussars position on its own. They fought bravely to help the Glosters, the Northumberland Fusiliers and the Royal Ulster Rifles.

The UN's subsequent pursuit into North Korea and Chinese intervention in support of the North brought the war to a stalemate. On 22 April 1951 three Chinese armies attacked the UN forces. Directly in their path lay the British 29th Independent Brigade holding the Imjin River from Choksong on the left to the junction of the Imjin and Hantan on the right. Supporting it were Centurion tanks of C Squadron 8th King's Royal Irish Hussars and the 25-pounders of the 45th Field Regiment Royal Artillery.

In the ensuing battle the 1st Battalion The Gloucestershire Regiment were cut off and some of the Centurions and three Filipino M24s attempted to reach them. The light tanks were knocked out by mines and blocked the road, while the Centurions were forced back. Attempts to rescue other units of the Brigade were more successful. For the Glosters there was to be no withdrawal.

Peter Ormrod was a hero of the Battle of the Imjin River and the Battle for Normandy. He first saw serious action with C Squadron, 8th Hussars in Korea in February 1951, when they were supporting the 1st Battalion, The Gloucestershire Regiment. The latter was moving onto Hill 327 overlooking the Han River east of Seoul. In his role as squadron second-in-command he moved forward with the Glosters on foot so that he could direct tank fire onto Chinese-held bunkers.

During the Battle of the Imjin River in April he found himself in temporary command of C Squadron. His tanks were soon under threat after the Chinese infiltrated British positions and stuck explosives on their side armour and tracks. Following the loss of several tanks he withdrew to form a more effective defensive perimeter.

Chinese troops tried to encircle Ormrod's tanks, but he led half the squadron to clear the gap. A tank following him had to machine-gun his vehicle to prevent Chinese soldiers attempting to climb aboard. He was wounded just as the enemy were driven away and his squadron leader arrived with the reserve tank troop. On one occasion they could see around 2,000 Chinese troops swarming down the western hillsides and their Centurion tanks simply ran over the enemy. For his actions he was awarded the Military Cross.

A total of 10 countries outside the Commonwealth sent armed units and 4 sent medical teams (of the 344,000 UN troops committed to the war 300,000 were from the USA). In particular, the Philippines provided a medium tank company and its forces were equipped with light tanks and self-propelled artillery. Filipino M24 Chaffees unsuccessfully tried to relieve the British Gloucestershire Regiment on the Imjin River. Turkish troops were considered the best of the smaller UN forces, fighting with distinction at Sinnimini and Osan, though they only provided an infantry brigade.

Britain's commitment to the fighting was a bit of a mixed bag that included a number of Second World War veterans. Among them were the Churchill Mk VII of C Squadron, 7th Royal Tank Regiment, which was the first British tank unit to arrive in Korea. These tanks were actually configured as Crocodile flamethrowers but the fuel trailers were discarded. (*Author's Collection*)

The 8th King's Royal Irish Hussars included Cromwell tanks, and this particular one was lost in Normandy in 1944. (*Author's Collection*)

Just visible on the left is a M4A3(76) HVSS supporting men of the Argyll and Sutherland Highlanders as they enter Chonju, 16 November 1950. This type of tank equipped Lord Strathcona's Horse, Canadian 2nd Armoured Regiment, which deployed to Korea with the Canadian 25th Infantry Brigade. (*Author's Collection*)

Although the British contribution to the war was relatively small, it packed a punch in the shape of the highly successful Centurion tank. This tank was developed at the end of the Second World War and entered service with the British Army in 1949. (*Author's Collection*)

The Centurion is an anomaly among British tank designs. In fact it was probably the most successful British tank ever with over 4,400 produced, of which 2,500 were exported. In Korea the accuracy of its 20-pounder gun and its agility won the Centurion acclaim among its crews. (*Author's Collection*)

The Daimler Dingo Scout Car, seen here, and the Universal Carrier were two more proven vehicles from the Second World War that were deployed by British and Commonwealth forces to Korea. These particular ones were photographed in Malaya during the Chinese-backed Communist emergency. (*Author's Collection*)

Tough-looking men from 41 Commando, Royal Marines planting demolition charges along railroad tracks of a Communist supply line, some 8 miles south of Songjin, 10 April 1951. (*Via Author*)

A British tank crew decorate their Centurion ready for Christmas in Korea. (*Author's Collection*)

The Centurion was not invulnerable; this particular one seems to have been caught by a mine. The force of the explosion that knocked it out was so great that a piece of the armour plating ended up twisted round the barrel. British troops plus their local mascot, a young Korean boy who is rigged out in their uniform, are inspecting the vehicle. (*Author's Collection*)

Commonwealth armour was not as well armed as the Pershing and the Patton with their powerful 90mm gun. Tanks such as this one from the 1st Marine Tank Battalion were deployed in support of the Turkish Brigade which lacked its own tanks. In all, four different Turkish brigades rotated through Korea. (*US DoD*)

Ethiopian troops being briefed in Korea in May 1951. Emperor Haile Salassie sent the 1st Kagnew (Conquerors) Battalion formed in August 1950 drawn from his Imperial Guard. Consisting of three rifle companies, they also had no armoured support. They arrived in Pusan on 7 May 1951 and fought alongside the US 32nd Infantry Regiment, 7th Infantry Division with distinction. (*Via Author*)

Kagnew gunners with US 105mm guns. During the course of the war the Ethiopians took part in hundreds of battles including the Iron Triangle and Pork Chop Hill engagements. In total they suffered 122 killed and 526 wounded. (*Via Author*)

Most Australian, British and Canadian Commonwealth units in Korea made use of the versatile Universal Carrier. This Australian Pattern Carrier Mk 2A has the Royal Air Force Roundel which was a recognition symbol adopted by some of the Commonwealth forces. The men are clearly enjoying a 'brew-up'. (*Australian Army*)

Australians inspecting what appears to be a Centurion armoured recovery vehicle. (*Author's Collection*)

A British Centurion crew conduct some housekeeping during a lull in the fighting. British tanks by 1952 rarely had the Allied white stars and markings were restricted to registration number, arm of service and the insignia of the 1st British Commonwealth Division (which consisted of three brigades). (*Author's Collection*)

Overall, the bulk of the armour supporting UN operations in Korea was from the USA. Here men of the US 3rd Rangers, 3rd Infantry Division, supported by M26 or M46 tanks, advance north of the Imjin River across the contested 38th Parallel. They were photographed on 11 April 1951 under Chinese mortar fire. (*US DoD*)

US infantry taking cover from in-coming Communist fire. (*US DoD*)

Another British Centurion tank *hors de combat*, apparently disabled by a mine somewhere in Korea. Notably, it has lost two of its nearside road wheels. (*Via Author*)

Chapter Six

Inchon Triumph

The daring amphibious assault on Inchon west of Seoul was to prove the turning point in the war. General Douglas MacArthur conceived of the landings as a way of breaking the Communist stranglehold on the South. This left hook would distract the NKPA by turning their flank and permit the UN forces trapped in the Pusan bridgehead to break out. Both US Army and Marine Corps armour was to play its part.

About 70,000 troops were transported from Pusan and Japan to Inchon. The armada of 260 ships comprised vessels from the USA, France, Britain, Canada, New Zealand and the Netherlands. On 15 September 1950 the USA launched the assault, which was intended to envelop the over extended enemy from the rear. Codenamed Operation Chromite, the first objective was the capture of the island of Wolmi-do, at the entrance to the port of Inchon. Once secured large numbers of troops could be brought forward, and the island would then act as a springboard for the invasion.

Spearheading the attack was the US 1st Marine Division; its 1st Tank Battalion consisted of a headquarters and service company, as well as three tank companies with fifteen M26 Pershing tanks. The 1st Amphibian Tractor Battalion was equipped with Landing Vehicle Tracked (LVT) known as amtracs. Also the US 7th Infantry Division included tank and engineer combat battalions and a reconnaissance battalion. The tank companies of the 73rd Tank Battalion had twenty M26 tanks, while the recognisance units had M24 light tanks and M8 and M20 armoured cars.

The Marines deployed both the LVT3(C) and the LVT(A)5 (Modified). The former was a post-war modification of the LVT3 (of which 2,962 were built) with a machine-gun turret and aluminium hatches over the troop compartment (hence the C). The latter was also a post-war modification of the LVT(A)5 with an improved bow, removal of the hull machine gun, access doors in the hull sides and the addition of a fully enclosed turret with a 75mm howitzer. The USA built 269 LVT(A)5, but they were too late to see action during the Second World War. Both vehicle types were involved in the Inchon landings with the US Marine Corps.

Communist defences so far behind their front lines were fairly weak. The key armoured units were the 42nd and 43rd Tank Regiments equipped with T-34/85s that were in the Seoul area. Most of the artillery defending Inchon comprised Soviet-supplied 76.2mm M1942 field guns which could also be used in an anti-tank role so were a threat to the Pershings.

The North Korean 226th Marine Regiment, consisting of around 2,000 men, manned the defences at the port. Further inland to the north-east Kimpo Airfield was held by the 2,500 troops of the 107th Security Regiment. At Yongdungp'o were elements of two rifle divisions, the 9th and 18th, numbering about 10,000. Units from the 31st and 42nd Divisions plus the 25th Rifle Brigade totalling at most 10,000 men held Seoul itself.

During the assault US fighters flew 2,533 sorties with 11 aircraft lost to enemy ground fire. Communist air cover was negligible and did not become threatening until the later use of the MiG-15. They had a number of Soviet-supplied Yakovlev and Lavochkin prop-driven fighters, but no jet fighters or bombers. The US Marine Air Wing alone dropped 5,328 bombs and 50,420lb of napalm during the operation. In the face of this onslaught the North Korean Air Force had severely limited air-defence capabilities.

The 1st Marine Tank Battalion stormed ashore with its M26s, M4A3 flamethrowers and M4A3 tank-dozers. Inland six T-34s of the NKPA's 42nd Tank Regiment heading for Inchon lost three of their number to Marine Corsair fighter bombers at Kanson-Ni and the rest to the advancing M26 Pershings. On 17 September the Pershings surprised another six tanks and killed up to 250 NKPA infantry for the cost of only 1 man wounded. The US 1st Marine Division was credited with knocking out a total of forty-four enemy tanks during the fighting. It did not lose a single tank to enemy armour during the operations, though several were victims of enemy infantry attacks and mines.

To the south one of the largest tank actions occurred during the UN's break out from the Pusan perimeter on 16 September designed to link up with the landings. The US 70th Tank Battalion, supporting the US 1st Cavalry Division of Task Force Lynch, claimed only one T-34 for the loss of two Shermans. The NKPA though lost an additional five T-34s to US bazooka teams. It took three days to gain a bridgehead on the far side of the Naktong River and begin the drive on Seoul. By 26 September Task Force Lynch had destroyed thirteen enemy tanks for the loss of two Shermans.

General MacArthur was wrong when he said Seoul would fall in five days – it took fourteen. The North Koreans had turned the city into a fortress and Seoul was recaptured on 27 September. The NKPA lost fifty T-34s during the Inchon campaign. Suddenly, the NKPA's armour was not having everything its own way. The US 7th Infantry Division then took part in a second amphibious assault, this time on the east coast, landing at Wonsan on 26 October and Iwon three days later.

Following the hugely successful amphibious assault at Inchon by the US 10th Corps, the US 8th Army pushed north along the western coast of Korea, while RoK's 1st Corps and the US 10th Corps advanced north via the eastern coast. On October 1950 the Chinese Army secretly crossed into North Korea to prop up the Communists. After the landing at Wonsan, the US 1st Marine Division part of 10th Corps engaged the Chinese 124th Division in early November and inflicted heavy casualties.

On 21 November, the 17th Infantry Regiment, US 7th Infantry Division reached the banks of the Yalu River, one of the northernmost advances of the UN during the course of the war. The Chinese then withdrew to lure the UN forces into a trap at the Chosin Reservoir. By 24 November the Marines had taken up positions on both sides of the reservoir. During the retreat from Chosin the 7th Infantry Division lost 2,657 killed and 354 wounded. The terrible ratio of dead to wounded shows the ferocity of the fighting.

By April 1951 the entire 8th Army was advancing north on a line stretching across the Korean peninsula, reaching the 38th Parallel the following month. The US 7th Infantry Division, assigned to 9th Corps, fought a fierce three-day battle culminating in the recapture of terrain that had been lost near the Hwachon Reservoir just over the 38th Parallel in North Korea. After taking the town bordering on the reservoir they cut off thousands of enemy troops.

The US invasion fleet gathered off the port of Inchon for Operation Chromite. This was a daring amphibious left-hand hook against the NKPA's flank. The patrolling aircraft is the Vought F4U Corsair readily identifiable by its inverted gull wing. (US DoD)

A pre-landing bombardment by cruisers, destroyers and rocket ships on 15 September 1950 softened the way for the US Marines assault forces. Also three flights of Marine Corsairs dropped napalm on Wolmi-do to burn down the vegetation and reveal enemy positions. These 16in guns actually belong to the USS *Missouri* bombarding Hungnam in December 1950. (*US DoD*)

The *Missouri* photographed the month before shelling North Korean communications at Ching Jin. It gives a vivid display of the weight of firepower the US Navy could drop onto a target. (*US DoD*)

From left to right, Brigadier General Courtney Whitney, General Douglas MacArthur, Commander in Chief of UN forces, and Major General Edward Almond observe the shelling of Inchon from the amphibious command ship USS *Mount McKinley* on 15 September 1950. (*US DoD*)

(*Opposite, top*) A US Landing Ship heading for the coast at Inchon. General Charles Willoughby, MacArthur's intelligence officer, was confident that the coastal defence batteries would be quickly destroyed sparing the fleet from heavy calibre gunfire, which included 76.2mm field guns. Blue and Red Beaches alone were deluged with 6,000 rockets. (*US DoD*)

(*Opposite, below*) Members of 3rd Platoon, Company H, 2nd Battalion, 5th Marines equipped with scaling ladders en route to Beach Green on the island of Wolmi-do, the gateway to Inchon harbour. (*US DoD*)

Marines of 3rd Platoon storm over the sea wall at Wolmi-do. The North Korean defenders had been stunned by the preliminary bombardment. (*US DoD*)

(*Opposite, top*) Marines move cautiously through the shattered buildings on Wolmi-do. By 1200hr on 15 September 1950 the 3rd Battalion, 5th Marines had finished mopping up resistance on the island and the neighbouring island of Sowolmi-do. (*US DoD*)

(*Opposite, below*) More US forces come ashore from a Landing Ship, while trucks and other 'soft skin' vehicles are just visible on the deck. (*US DoD*)

Four bulky Landing Ship Tank vessels disgorge men and vehicles onto Red Beach at Inchon, 15 September 1950. A total of eight re-supply LSTs beached there at 1900hr. (*US DoD*)

Relaxed looking Marines gathered in front of a blazing tobacco warehouse in central Inchon. Although the port was way behind the North Korean lines, it still had a sizeable garrison drawn from various NKPA units. (*US DoD*)

Supplies are unloaded from a ship into an amphibious DUKW in Inchon harbour. This vehicle had proved its worth during the amphibious landings of the Second World War. (*US DoD*)

US troops make use of North Korean barricades on the streets of Seoul. The North Koreans had turned the city into a fortress defended by 10,000 men supported by 2 tank regiments. (*US DoD*)

Pershing tanks of the 1st Marine Tank Battalion push through Seoul while South Korean infantry and irregulars round up Communist prisoners, 26 September 1950. (*US DoD*)

In Seoul the Americans found themselves up against elements of three NKPA infantry divisions which fought stubbornly to hold onto the city. (*US DoD*)

Men of the US 1st Marine Division pose for the cameras in liberated Seoul on Korean bicycles; behind them are two Pershings from the 1st Tank Battalion that provided vital tank support in the face of NKPA T-34s. (*US DoD*)

General MacArthur and his senior staff officer Brigadier General Courtney Whitney examine a knocked out North Korean T-34 following the landings. General Willoughby was anxious about the location of the NKPA's 105th Tank Division, as this was a threat to Operation Chromite. He was unaware that the division had regrouped in Kumchon where it was being re-equipped with new T-34/85 tanks, SU-76 self-propelled guns and armoured personnel carriers. (*US DoD*)

US Marines launching 4.5in rockets against enemy positions. The rapid expansion of the Inchon/Seoul bridgehead made a North Korean withdrawal inevitable. (*US DoD*)

A Marine sniper and his spotter from 1st Marine Division work together to pick off enemy troops. Although the NKPA was driven back it was far from defeated. (*US DoD*)

The remains of a Communist roadblock. China watched the UN's rapid advance northward with alarm. (*US DoD*)

The successful Inchon landings were followed by an amphibious assault on Wonsan, on North Korea's eastern coast opposite Pyongyang, 26 October 1950. This photo shows the dock facilities and warehouses at Wonsan being attacked by US B26 bombers. (*US DoD*)

Chapter Seven

Korean Swansong

The bulk of the UN's armoured fighting vehicles (AFVs) deployed to Korea were designed and built by the USA. Many of them dated from the Second World War and in some cases were pressed into service from reserve stock. Notably the M24 Chaffee light tank saw service at the end of the North West European and Pacific campaigns in 1945. Originally designed as a replacement for the M3-M5 series during the Second World War, it was a fast, efficient reconnaissance vehicle and between April 1944 and June 1945 4,070 were built. The most important feature compared to its predecessors was the use of a 75mm rather than a 37mm gun.

These were the first US tanks committed to battle in Korea. Three M24s fought a number of T-34/85s on 10 July 1950 knocking out one enemy tank while losing two of their own number. In fact, up against the NKPA's T-34/85 they did not fair at all well. At Pusan they were more useful as dug-in self-propelled artillery. M8 Greyhound armoured cars equipped the reconnaissance companies of the US Infantry Divisions. Like the M24 Chaffee, it was totally outclassed by the T-34/85 and did not prove very successful in Korea.

The M4A3 Sherman HVSS (Horizontal Volute Spring Suspension) armed with a heavier 76mm gun had also seen service towards the end of the Second World War. Other variants deployed in Korea included the M4A3 HVSS POA-CWS-H5 flamethrower and the M4A3 tank-dozer. Each tank company had a tank-dozer for earth-moving and road-improvement tasks.

The powerful M26 Pershing tank armed with a 90mm gun arrived late on the scene at the end of the Second World War. About 200 were built, though most did not see action. M26s of the Provisional Tank Platoon were the first US medium tank unit in Korea. The tank's debut in Korea was inauspicious as the first three deployed were abandoned after their retreat was cut off. The follow-on M46 Patton likewise armed with a 90mm gun provided the mainstay of US armoured forces in Korea, along with the M4 and M26.

Similarly, the M32B1 tracked recovery vehicle proved vital in Korea for rescuing stranded tanks, often the victims of Korea's precarious roads. Being well armoured this vehicle was valuable for recovery operations in combat areas.

There were many other Second World War vintage AFVs used in Korea, including the M7B1 105mm howitzer motor carriage. To facilitate hill-side indirect fire the M7B2 conversion allowed a greater degree of howitzer elevation. The M37 105mm howitzer motor carriage was based on the M24 chassis and entered service in the closing days of the Second World War. It saw action with US field artillery battalions in Korea. During the Korean War self-propelled artillery tended to be termed 'tanks'.

The M40 155mm gun motor carriage using the M4A3 chassis along with the M37 provided the backbone of the self-propelled artillery. The M41 howitzer motor carriage armed with an 8in howitzer was also based on the M24 Chaffee and during the Second World War earned the nickname 'Gorilla'. The M43 8in howitzer motor carriage firing in a direct role was the weapon most feared by the Communists during positional warfare. They were so effective that they were guaranteed to attract counter battery fire immediately. This meant they would only fire several rounds before moving firing positions. Employed in small numbers, these were a weapon of last resort against particularly stubborn positions.

Deployed during the Second World War, the M15A1 mounted a 37mm gun and twin 50cal machine guns. Although a US vehicle, it was also used by other members of the multinational forces, including the Turkish Army. Another veteran, the M16 multiple gun motor carriage, was known as the 'Grinder' or 'Meat Chopper' because of its quad 50 machine guns mounted on the M3 half-track. Like so many anti-aircraft guns it was often used in a ground support role to devastating effect. The M19 gun motor carriage nicknamed the 'Flak-wagon' consisted of twin 40mm guns mounted on the M24 Chaffee light tank chassis. In Korea due to the vulnerability of its open fighting compartment it became known as the 'Rolling Coffin'.

The M39 armoured utility vehicle was used extensively in Korea for personnel carrying, supply and MEDVAC roles. It was also used to mount the M55 quad 50 or the 81mm mortar. As the open-topped M39 was found to be vulnerable to mortar and shell fire, in the closing weeks of the war the enclosed M75 armoured personnel carrier was used for supply tasks and was nicknamed the 'Lifesaver'. It proved particularly valuable during the battles for Pork Chop Hill.

Thanks to Stalin, the NKPA deployed two types of AFV, the T-34 tank and the SU-76 self-propelled gun. The venerable T-34/85 is reputedly the best tank of the Second World War; the armoured sides and front glacis plate were sloped to deflect shells effectively, while the diesel engine a massive 38.8 litre, 500 Brake Horse Power V12 gave tremendous torque and importantly for the crew reduced the risk of fire. The 76mm and the later 85mm were much larger than equivalent allied tank guns. The NKPA started off with about 150 of these vehicles, which ensured their initial victory.

In Korea the T-34 served the North Koreans well, but it was vulnerable to air attack, particularly napalm and the 90mm anti-tank guns of the Pershing and Patton. Eventually, they were to field three armoured brigades equipped with T-34. In total the NKPA committed around 240 such tanks to the war, the equivalent of 2 whole armoured divisions.

During the Second World War the Soviets lost faith in the utility of light tanks, so decided to employ their T-60 light tank chassis as the basis for a self-propelled gun mounting a 76.2mm anti-tank gun. The resulting lightly armoured SU-76 was deemed unsuitable as an anti-tank vehicle and was switched to the infantry support role. The NKPA used it in this role and started the war with about 120 in its infantry divisions. The relatively light armour and lack of overhead protection for the fighting compartment made it vulnerable when out-ranged by its opponents. It was replaced in the Soviet inventory by the SU-85.

For whatever reason Stalin did not see fit to supply the NKPA with armour equipped with heavier guns such as the SU-100, ISU-122/152 or the IS-2. All of these would have presented the UN with major problems and posed a real threat to the Pershing and Patton. In any case, the North Koreans grasp of mechanised warfare was rudimentary at best and the T-34 was largely foolproof. Indeed, it would continue to see combat around the world after the Korean War, especially in Africa and the Middle East.

(*Opposite, top*) A Sherman tank of the 70th Tank Battalion serving with the US 1st Cavalry Division. The Detroit Arsenal built 1,445 M4A3 (76mm) HVSS between August and December 1944 in an effort to give the Sherman greater firepower during the closing months of the Second World War. This was one of the few US tank types available for operations in Korea. (*Via Author*)

(*Opposite, below*) These NKPA T-34s were victims of US airpower. Caught in the path of the US 24th Infantry Division they were blasted out of the way by the US 5th Air Force using napalm. Intriguingly, the tanks are face to face for some reason. (*US DoD*)

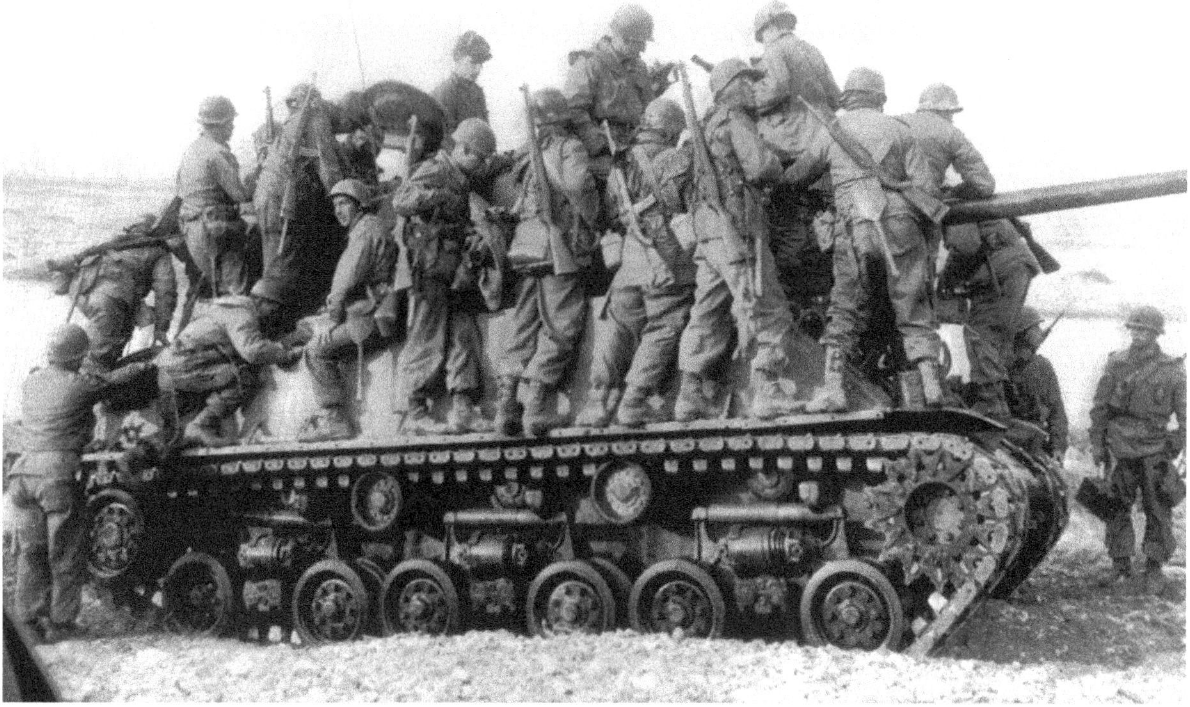

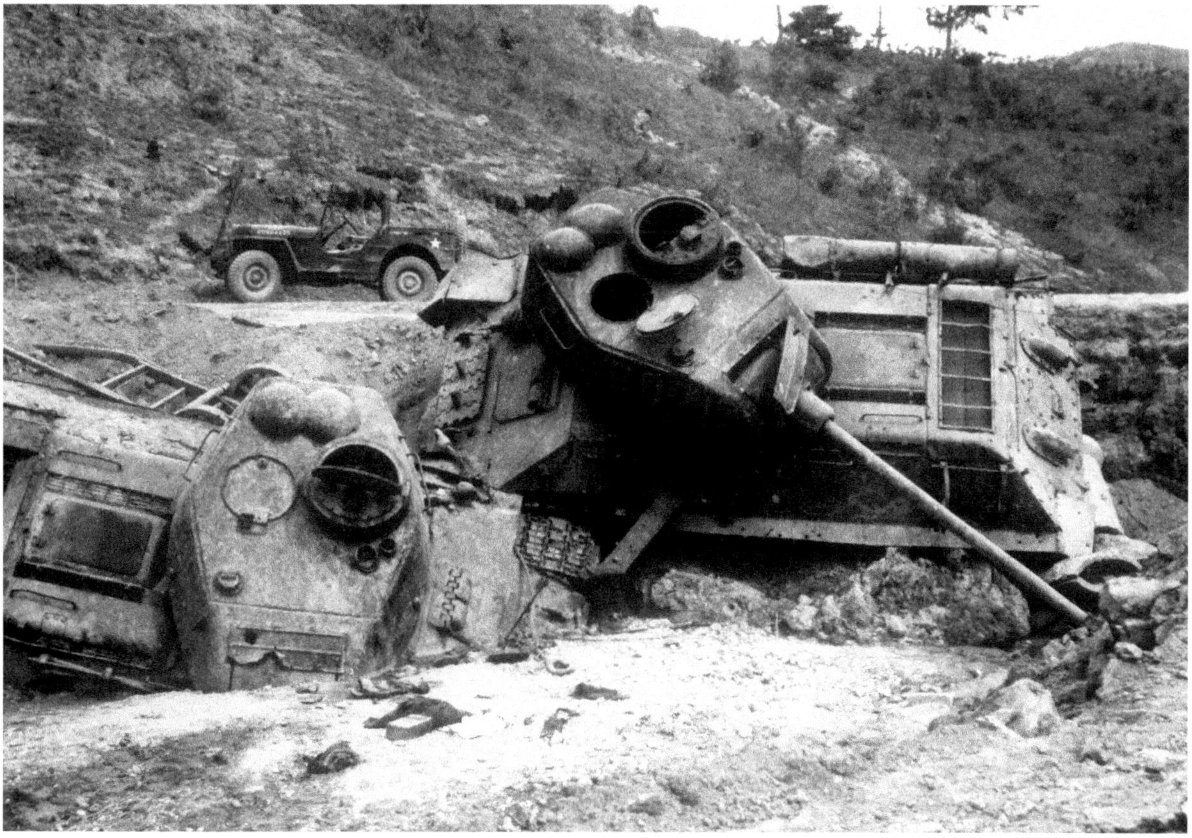

A shattered British Cromwell destroyed during the Battle of Imjin River. This tank was under armoured and under gunned, a common problem with Britain's armoured forces. (*Via Author*)

This burned out Sherman from the 89th Tank Battalion (formerly the 8072nd Medium Tank Battalion), US 25th Infantry Division, is deemed to be beyond recovery. A demolition squad from the 65th Engineer Battalion is placing dynamite under the tracks to ensure the tank does not fall into enemy hands. (*US DoD*)

Now there is a challenge for the engineers. Another Sherman from the US 1st Cavalry Division has got itself in a bit of a jam after this bridge near Yangzi gave way on 28 January 1951. Men from the 8th Engineer Battalion have inserted a log to brace the bridge until the vehicle can be retrieved. (*US DoD*)

This Second World War vintage M7B1 105mm howitzer motor carriage belongs to B Battery, 300th Armored Field Artillery Battalion, 10th Corps. Some of these vehicles were modified to increase the elevation of the gun from +35 to +65 degrees to improve indirect fire. This modification was known as the M7B2. (*US DoD*)

What appears to be a Sherman M4A3 (105mm) HVSS fitted with a dozer blade is involved in the fighting for the South Korean capital Seoul. Over 3,300 Sherman HVSS were built armed with the 105mm gun during 1944–5. (*US DoD*)

Each tank company in Korea had a tank-dozer to help with heavy moving tasks. This one is an M4A3(76)W HVSS tank-dozer with the M2 dozer blade serving with the 9th Tank Company, 9th Infantry regiment, US 2nd Infantry Division. (*US DoD*)

A British Centurion pushes through the snow, its crew on alert for any trouble. This tank should have seen service during the Second World War, but was not ready in time. In Korea its abilities won it widespread renown. (*Author's Collection*)

A Sherman crossing the Han River as it retreats from Seoul following the Chinese intervention on 4 January 1951. It was the very last tank to leave the city and the pontoon bridge was destroyed shortly after. (*US DoD*)

Two US Shermans, belonging to the 5th Regimental Combat Team, moving up to the front in the Kumchun area in early October 1950. In terms of firepower and profile the Sherman was eclipsed by the M26 and M46. (*US DoD*)

Members of the 2nd Engineer Combat Battalion sweep the road for anti-tank mines on 16 March 1951. Communist mines were always an ever-present danger for UN tanks deployed to Korea. Note how the vehicles have prudently pulled off the road until the check is complete. (*US DoD*)

Another mine-clearing operation. This time the soldier is from the 77th Engineer Company and has already partially uncovered a large roadside mine. (*US DoD*)

A Marine bulldozer is working on constructing a bridge at Koto-ri. (*US DoD*)

After the British Centurion's success in Korea it was to go on and serve the Israeli Defence Force during the Arab-Israeli Wars. (*Author's Collection*)

Chapter Eight

Turning the Tide

A survey conducted below the 38th Parallel in October 1950 counted 239 destroyed or abandoned T-34 tanks and 74 SU-76 self-propelled guns compared to 60 knocked-out US tanks. It claimed UN tank fire accounted for 39 tanks (16 per cent), rocket launchers 13 (5 per cent) and air strikes 102 (43 per cent) with napalm accounting for 60 (25 per cent) of the total. It does not record what happened to the rest, presumably victims of mines.

The USA had finally got its combination of armour, anti-tank weapons and air power (napalm was found to be effective against the T-34) right. Between 5 July and 25 November 1950 the 6147th Tactical Control Squadron flew 4,902 combat sorties claiming 436 enemy tanks, 785 trucks and 1,547 miscellaneous vehicles destroyed. This was a little optimistic.

The US Air Force (USAF) in the first two years of the war was to claim 1,134 AFVs, against 121 destroyed by ground weapons. This was more AFVs than the NKPA deployed throughout the whole war. Intelligence sources estimated that 242 T-34s had been committed to the battles in South Korea and that by September 1950 almost all of them had been destroyed. Total US tanks losses were recorded at 136 vehicles, of which 70 per cent were lost to mines (up by 50 per cent from the Second World War).

During the Korean War the UN forces flew a colossal 1,040,708 aerial sorties, second only in tempo to the Vietnam War. The US Far East Air Force had 350 combat ready planes at the start of hostilities, which quickly wrested air supremacy from the 110 North Korean piston-driven combat aircraft. The first encounter occurred on 27 June 1950 when three North Korean Yak-3 fired on four US jets covering the air evacuation from Kimpo and Suwon. All three were downed, followed by four more later in the day. In one day the USA destroyed one-sixth of the entire North Korean fighter force.

From late 1950 the Communists made strenuous attempts to gain control of the air from the more experienced UN pilots. The futility of this soon showed in their losses. For the loss of 114 planes, the UN destroyed or damaged 2,136 Communist aircraft, including 838 MiG-15s – there were another 177 probables. During the closing stages of the war 13 MiGs were being shot down for every US F-86.

In the first five months of 1951 the F-86 Sabre 4th Wing flew 3,550 sorties and claimed 22 victories; not a single Sabre was shot down by MiGs, though a number were lost to accidents. The Soviet MiG-15 jet fighter first appeared over Korea in late 1950, with initially some fifty aircraft flown by Chinese and Soviet pilots in support of the North Koreans. The first all-jet battle in history took place on 8 November 1950 when a US pilot shot down the first MiG. Despite the MiG-15's presence, the US F-86 Sabre achieved almost indisputable dominance over the skies of Korea, North and South. USAF claimed a total of 900 enemy aircraft, of which 792 were MiG-15s destroyed by Sabres. Sabre pilot Captain Joseph McConnell became a fighter ace with 16 kills. UN forces, though, did not have it all their own way. Operation Strangle designed to cut North Korean supply lines cost the UN 343 aircraft lost and 290 damaged.

During June 1951 the Communists grew more confident and in some fierce engagements succeeded in downing several Sabres. The explanation for the increased effectiveness of the MiG fighter units was the arrival in Manchuria from March 1951 onwards of Czech, Polish and Russian pilots on three-month combat tours. At this stage Soviet Air Force MiGs were repainted in Chinese People's Air Force markings, but later MiGs openly displaying the plain red star insignia of the Soviets were encountered.

The Soviet 64th Fighter Aviation Corps was sent secretly to fight for North Korea in November 1950. Most of the pilots were veterans or aces of the Second World War. They claimed over 1,300 UN aircraft while losing 345 of their own. Among these Soviet pilots were sixteen aces, with the top scorer being Evgeni Pepelyaev with twenty-three kills. His closet rival was Captain Nikolay Sutyagin.

Sutyagin fought as a fighter pilot during both the Second World War and the Korean War. He was one of the top fighter aces fighting alongside the Chinese and North Koreans. He claimed 15 F-86 Sabres, 2 F-84 Thunderjets, 2 P-80 Shooting Stars and 2 Gloster Meteors shot down. He reportedly flew 149 combat missions resulting in 66 aerial engagements during which he personally shot down a total of 21 enemy aircraft (plus 2 others shot down in a group). Sutyagin was awarded the Order of Lenin, three Orders of the Red Banner, Order of the Patriotic War First Class and a Hero of the Soviet Union.

While the Soviet pilots thought the MiG-15 was a superior aircraft, its engine had a nasty habit of cutting out during a sharp turn. They thought the US F-80 Shooting Star was not very good; the F-84 Thunderjet average; the F-86 Sabre excellent. Alexandr Pavolich Smortzkow finished the war with 12 victories consisting of 5 Australian Meteors, 5 US B-29s and 2 F-86s. Smortzkow recalled, 'One day we attacked a group of Australian Gloster Meteors. They were big, easy targets for us. My friend Oskin and I destroyed five Meteors during this one fight.'

Communist pilots had few successes, however, as their gunnery was often poor. In dogfights MiGs were not infrequently seen to spin out and crash, probably because the aircraft had no provision for G-suits and was rather unstable giving no warning of an impending stall and had a slow roll rate. By the time of the ceasefire in July 1953 there were 297 Sabres in Korea facing around 950 Sino-Korean MiGs. During the conflict F-86 pilots claimed to have destroyed 792 MiGs in air-to-air combat for the loss of 78 Sabres – a phenomenal 10 : 1 kills-to-loss ratio.

Crucially, the North Korean, Chinese and Soviet air forces had little bearing on the ground war; rather they spent much of their time engaged in aerial dogfights. Fighting enemy jets was one thing, but pressing home attacks on well-defended ground forces often with numerous anti-aircraft guns was another matter. The upshot was that the NKPA's armour lacked fighter cover as well as fighter bomber and bomber support.

The North Koreans had no real answer to the airpower that the UN forces were able to bring to bear. The NKPA's tanks were particularly vulnerable to air attack. This US Grumman F9F Panther jet is rocketing a road bridge somewhere in Korea and operating from the carrier USS *Bon Homme Richard*. The Panther performed well in Korea where it formed the bulk of the US Navy and US Marine Corps carrier jet force. (*US DoD*)

US Navy Skyraiders from the USS *Valley Forge* launching 5in rockets at North Korean field positions, 24 October 1950. The Douglas AD Skyraider appeared too late to take part in the Second World War and received its baptism of fire over Korea. (*US DoD*)

North Korean supply trains go up in a ball of flames. Communist lines of communication were soon paralysed by such attacks. (*US DoD*)

Two blazing NKPA T-34s near Yongsan, 1 September 1950. These tanks were resisting the advance of the US 1st Marine Division and the US 2nd Infantry Division as they pushed on the Naktong River. The T-34s look as if they were fleeing air attack, note the turret of the one in the foreground is facing rearward. (*US DoD*)

Yet another NKPA T-34, this one seems to have been abandoned by its crew. Over 40 per cent of North Korean tank losses were due to air strikes, and of these a quarter destroyed using napalm. (*Via Author*)

Men from the US 24th Infantry Division examine three T-34s knocked out by USAF, early October 1950. A Sherman belonging to the 6th Tank Battalion is just visible between the two T-34s at the top of the ravine. A fourth wrecked T-34 was found hidden in the tunnel. (US DoD)

North Korean lines of communication were swiftly cut making it almost impossible to move men and supplies. Getting replacement tanks and assault guns to the front became increasingly difficult. Two spans of this bridge over the Han River were brought down. (*US DoD*)

US Navy F4U Corsair fighters operating off the USS *Philippine Sea* with Navy Task Force 77 on the south-west coast of Korea. Wartime production of the Corsair continued until 1952. (*US DoD*)

A row of F-86 Sabres, June 1951. Initially, this aircraft flew with impunity, but the arrival of foreign pilots operating with the Chinese Air Force resulted in some losses and hampered Operation Strangle, the attempt to cut Communist supply lines completely. (*US DoD*)

Dwight D. Eisenhower on a visit to Korea. Once president he moved to pressure China to accept an armistice rather than see the war spiral out of control. (*US DoD*)

(*Opposite, top*) A flight of USAF B-26 Douglas Invader light bombers on a training mission over Japan. (*US DoD*)

(*Opposite, below*) Men of the US 1st Marine Aircraft Wing offer a Christmas message for the North Korean and Chinese Armies, which is about to be delivered by a Grumman F7F Tigercat twin-engined fighter. Although designed as a carrier-based aircraft due to it size and weight, it was mainly used by the US Marines as a land-based fighter. (*US DoD*)

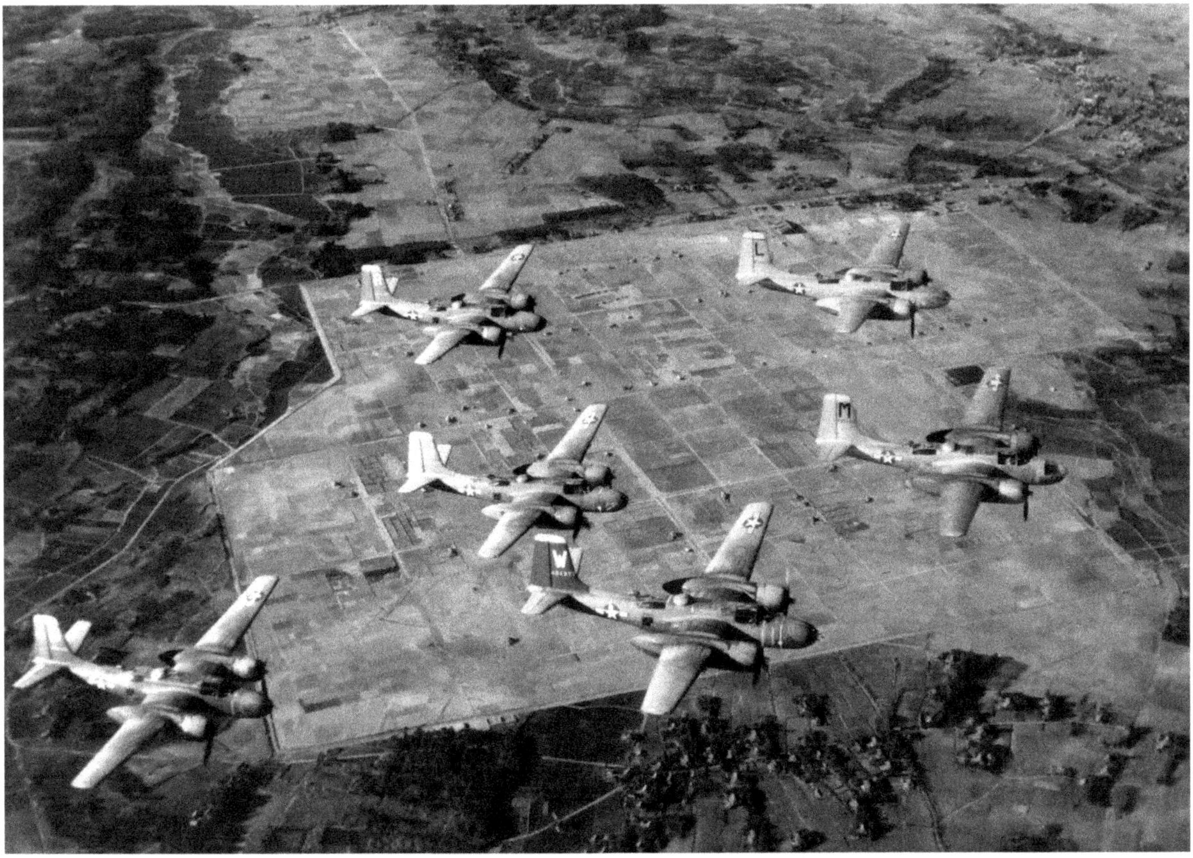

30
MERRY
XMAS
FROM 1st
MAW

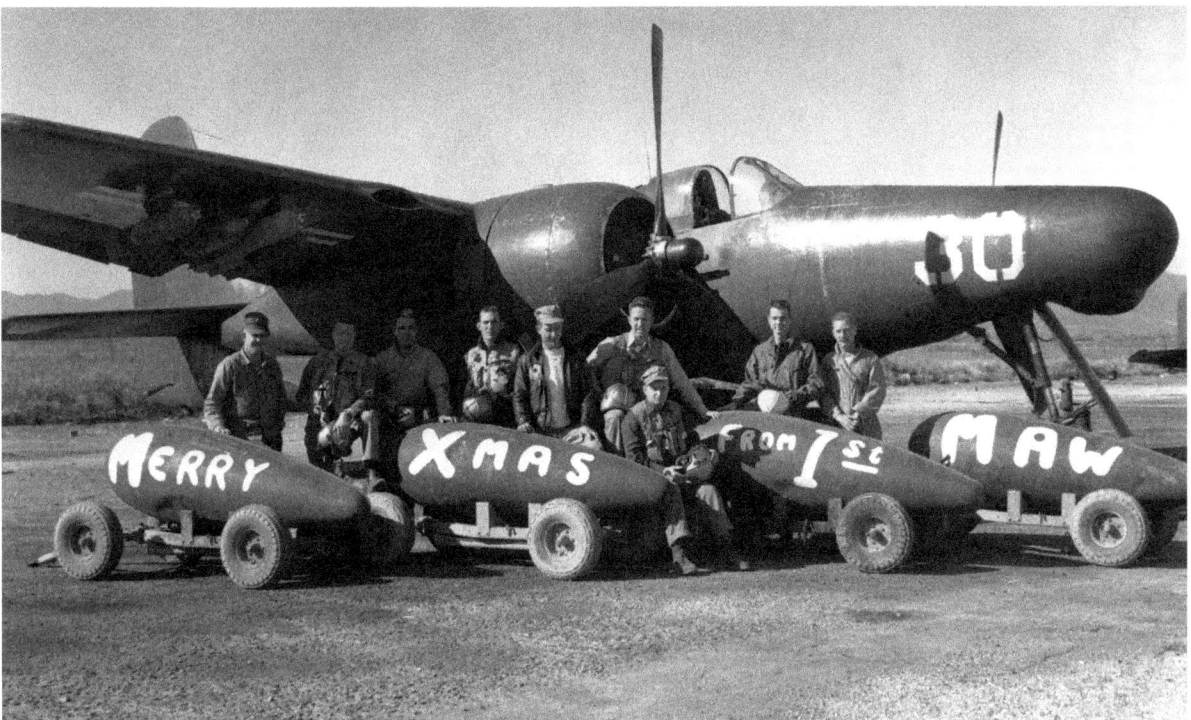

Devastation west of the Naktong near Waegwan caused by US B-29 bombers on 16 August 1950 when they delivered 3,400 500lb bombs. (*US DoD*)

(*Opposite, top*) North Korea's ability to keep it tanks and trucks operating on the front line was greatly hampered when the Chosen oil refinery at Wonsan was bombed in four attacks in July and August by B-29s. The refinery supplied almost all the finished petroleum products for the NKPA. (*US DoD*)

(*Opposite, below*) A Royal Australian Hawker Sea Fury, which was capable of delivering bombs, rockets and mines. In Korea this aircraft proved to be an excellent ground-attack platform as well as an air-to-air fighter. On at least two occasions it triumphed over the MiG-15. (*Australian Navy*)

The first major conventional war for helicopters was Korea, where such aircraft as the Sikorsky S-51/H-5 (seen here) and Bell 47 were used for casevac and reconnaissance purposes. Four helicopters accompanied the 1st Provisional US Marine Brigade to South Korea in 1950 and the first-ever heli evacuation of US casualties was performed by Marine VMO-6 helicopters on 4 August 1950. (*Author's Collection*)

The Bell 47 carried two stretcher casualties in external pods for lifting wounded to the Mobile Army Surgical Hospitals or MASH. (*Author's Collection*)

The success of the UN/US airpower had its drawbacks. Pontoon bridges had continually to be built to ferry tanks and other vehicles over Korea's numerous rivers. (*US DoD*)

Chapter Nine

First Spring Offensive

For at least two-and-a-half months after the outbreak of the Korean War, the nine-month-old Communist government of the People's Republic of China felt it could stand by and watch events unfold. Once Kim Il-Sung's tanks had reached Pusan victory seemed assured for the North. The only unknown was how the international community would react to the forcible reunification of the two Koreas.

The UN greeted the news of the successful landings by the US Marines at Inchon in mid-September 1950 with relief. The defenders of the Pusan perimeter having broken out of their Communist cage shattered the North Koreans and barged them back to the 38th Parallel and beyond. By the end of October UN forces had captured Pyongyang, the North Korean capital, and were pushing towards both the Chinese and Soviet borders.

Within the space of just four weeks the balance of victory and defeat had been completely reversed, although the UN was to become a victim of its own success. With UN forces now just 150 miles from the Yalu River marking the border between North Korea and China, the Chinese considered themselves to be under threat. They had every reason to feel this as the UN had refused to recognise the People's Republic of China following the defeat of the Nationalists. The last thing they wanted was Western forces on their doorstep.

The Communists under Mao were still consolidating their control across China and the rump North Korea state provided a convenient buffer with Manchuria. Nonetheless, ever the pragmatist, during July 1950 Mao had massed 116,000 troops in Manchuria and at the end of August this figure had risen to 250,000. By October, with UN forces pushing north to the Yalu, Chinese troop numbers in Manchuria were approaching 750,000. Ironically, the UN, keen not to provoke China, had forbidden reconnaissance flights north of the Yalu.

During 14–16 October 1950 the first of what were dubbed the People's Volunteers began to filter by night across the Yalu bridges. By 1 November China had inserted 18 divisions, some 180,000 men, into North Korea. Over the next few weeks over 300,000 sneaked over the border.

UN commander General Douglas MacArthur believed that China's warnings of intervention were bluff and he was denied any intelligence that might have swayed him otherwise. Instead, MacArthur was completely unaware of the massive Chinese build-up. Nonetheless, General Ridgway recalled, 'Well-camouflaged tanks were observed, new troop units, and anti-aircraft batteries.' These warning signs were ignored.

Elements of the South Korean 7th Regiment from RoK's 6th Infantry Division became the first unit to reach the Yalu River on 26 October. The following day after a vicious close-quarter battle fought in the freezing winter weather the South Koreans were overwhelmed by Chinese troops. Then on 28 October the rest of the 6th Division suffered the same fate. Three other South Korean divisions flanking the US 8th Army were sent reeling under the weight of the attack, leaving the Americans exposed with a gap on their right.

Tanks of the US 8th Cavalry Regiment were sent to try and save the day. Near the small town of Unsan on 1 November the regiment's 3rd Battalion was surrounded by hordes of Chinese infantry frantically blowing bugles and whistles. The following day other units of the 8th Cavalry Regiment, which had escaped the Chinese, retreated along the narrow twisting mountain road leading from Unsan; they were ambushed by the People's Volunteers armed with just submachine guns and grenades. Unsan cost the 8th Cavalry over half its manpower, 12 howitzers, 9 tanks and 125 trucks and 12 recoilless rifles.

The Chinese finally broke off their attacks on 7 November and the UN forces withdrew across the Chongchon River. MacArthur assumed that the Chinese had simply made a show of strength as a warning and that would be the end of the matter. Nonetheless, he had got permission to bomb the Yalu bridges and to launch a counterattack. The 8th Army under Lieutenant General Walton Walker, his command included four US and four South Korean divisions, the 27th British Commonwealth Brigade and the Turkish Brigade, was to advance from the Chongchon.

On the night of 25/26 November, the UN forces marching west of the mountains were hit by a marauding mass of 180,000 Chinese soldiers. The three South Korean divisions at Tokchon on the 8th Army's right flank disintegrated and the US 2nd Infantry Division lost over 4,000 of its 5,000 men killed. The UN once again was forced back on the Chongchon, and by 5 December Pyongyang was evacuated and by the 13th the UN having retreated 120 miles in ten days reached the Imjin River.

Shortly after China entered the Korean War, the People's Volunteer 9th Army infiltrated the north-eastern part of North Korea and surprised the US 10th Corps in the Chosin Reservoir area. A fierce seventeen-day battle was fought in the bitter winter weather. From 27 November to 13 December 1950 some 30,000 UN troops dubbed 'The Chosin Few' under Major General Edward Almond were encircled by 60,000 Chinese troops under General Song Shilun.

Hungnam became a bridgehead that fought off repeated Chinese attacks. Its sanctuary eluded over half of the men of the US 7th Infantry Division who were caught in the area of the Chosin Reservoir. Of 1,000 men who managed to fight their way down to Hagaru on the reservoir's southern tip on 2 December 615 were unfit for further combat.

The UN troops managed to break out and thanks to the superior firepower of their tanks and artillery inflicted terrible losses on the Chinese. While the UN suffered about 4,600 casualties, the Chinese lost up to 50 per cent of their force. The evacuation of the US 10th Corps from the port of Hungnam marked the complete withdrawal of UN troops from North Korea. The US 1st Marine Division and Regimental Combat Team 31 were awarded the Presidential Unit citation for their tenacity during the battle. The Korean War Chosin Reservoir Battle memorial was unveiled by the USMC Commandant at Camp Pendleton in 2010.

The winter of 1951 saw the Chinese PLA intervene in the Korean War in support of North Korea. Surrounded by snow, a Pershing of the US 6th Tank Battalion engages enemy targets. Despite the UN's firepower they were unable to hold the massed numbers of the PLA at bay. (*US DoD*)

These men of the Heavy Mortar Company, US 7th Infantry Regiment have gone native cooking rice in their foxhole in the Kagae-dong area, 7 December 1950. The Chinese attack caught men such as this completely off guard and few believed that the Chinese intervention would be long term. (*US DoD*)

US troops hitch a ride on an M46 Patton tank. The main difference between this and the earlier M26 Pershing is the small additional road wheel visible at the rear. (*Via Author*)

Frostbitten marines awaiting orders to try and fight their way out of the Chosin Reservoir area. US forces were trapped here during November–December 1950. (*US DoD*)

The winter conditions were appalling, note the snow chains on this truck's tyres. Its crew is laying grit to try and stop the road freezing over. (*US DoD*)

US Marines move forward after close air support flushed out the enemy from their hill-side positions near Hagaru-ri on 26 December 1950. A bulldozer is blocking the road and in the far distance the outline of a Pershing tank can just be made out. (*US DoD*)

Lieutenant General Matthew B. Ridgway, commanding the US 8th Army, standing on the left gives the order to dismantle the pontoon bridge after the last of the UN forces were evacuated from Seoul on 4 January 1951. (*US DoD*)

A wounded soldier from the 35th Regiment, US 25th Infantry Division is hoisted onto a Sherman from the 89th Tank Battalion for evacuation, 7 March 1951. He was one of the lucky ones to escape the advancing PLA and NKPA. (*US DoD*)

Bulldozers such as this one were vital in keeping the roads open in the path of the retreating UN forces. Rockslides and heavy snow were as much a problem as enemy action. (*US DoD*)

Once the Chinese entered the war it became vital to cut the bridges over the Yalu River. This photograph shows USAF wrecking three parallel railway bridges over the Han south-west of Seoul. Such bridges were bombed early in the war to slow the advance of the NKPA. (*US DoD*)

US B-26 bombers hitting a mining complex near Changdo. The NKPA became increasingly reliant on the Chinese for raw materials as a result of this bombing campaign. (*US DoD*)

It was only once the Chinese had reached the end of their rudimentary supply lines and in the face of UN firepower that their advance slackened. The M40 gun motor carriage married a 155mm gun to the HVSS chassis and the M43 (seen here) an 8in howitzer to the same chassis. The latter was often used in a direct-fire support role with devastating results. (*US DoD*)

Lieutenant General Hodge commanding US 9th Corps poses with an M41 self-propelled gun about to fire the 75,000th shell on 25 June 1951. On his right is Brigadier William N. Gilmore, Commanding General Corps Artillery. On 24 April 1951 the 92nd Armored Field Artillery Battalion equipped with M41s fought off a Chinese attack killing 179 enemy for the loss of 4 dead and 11 wounded. (US DoD)

A gunner of the Tank Company, 5th Regimental Combat Team, US 24th Infantry Division, engages Chinese troops with a .50 calibre machine gun, mid-July 1951. The Chinese relied on weight of numbers rather than armour and fire support. (US DoD)

Chapter Ten

The Static War

Lieutenant General Matthew B. Ridgway took charge of the 8th Army after Lieutenant General Walton H. Walker was killed in a road accident on 23 December 1950. Also 10th Corps came under his command. There was to be no respite for Ridgway or his troops. The Chinese attacked again on 31 December with 400,000 men supported by 100,000 North Koreans who swarmed across the 38th Parallel. The South Korean forces melted away and 8th Army was forced to abandon Seoul on 4 January 1951. UN forces were once again driven back 275 miles and lost 13,000 men and large quantities of equipment.

Only when the Chinese ran out of supplies did they come to a halt, their long and exposed lines of communication soon pounded by UN jets that had command of the skies. The UN Air Force, which since 18 December included the powerful US F-86 Sabre jet fighter, did a great deal to protect the 8th Army during its miserable winter withdrawal.

During February two PLA and a North Korean army, employing massed 'human wave' tactics for the first time, surged toward Wonju. In the face of the UN's firepower and appalling casualties the Chinese were forced to withdraw back over the 38th Parallel having lost Seoul. The UN then launched a series of counterattacks with Operations Thunderbolt, Roundup and Killer.

Undeterred, on 22 April 1951 the Chinese spent four hours shelling UN positions, then 475,000 Communist troops massed in and around the 'Iron Triangle' launched phase one of the First Spring Offensive. The main obstacle to the Chinese advance was the heroic resistance by the 29th British Independent Brigade. The epic stand by the Glosters at the Imjin River broke the Chinese impetus. In a week the Chinese gained just 35 miles of territory at the cost of 70,000 men, while UN losses stood at 7,000.

In the second phase of their spring offensive, which started on 15 May, Chinese casualties reached even more staggering heights with the loss of 90,000 men. The attack ground to a halt five days later having smashed the South Korean 3rd Corps at Inje. UN counterattacks soon overran any gains and reached the 38th Parallel again.

The Chinese realised that victory over a mechanised, mobile, well-equipped and determined modern army could not be achieved by wave upon suicidal wave of disposable human beings. Nor could numbers alone make up for primitive logistics, inadequate communications and poor supply and training. Communist communications and supply dumps in North Korea were systematically devastated by aerial bombardment.

By November 1951 the Chinese and North Koreans were defending static defensive fortifications against an enemy, which although it had superior firepower had little desire to suffer yet more casualties. The war had reached its third and final stage – one of stalemate. The Chinese built a 14-mile-deep defensive system to protect them against UN artillery barrages and air strikes. Both sides created such strong defensive lines that neither had any real hope of achieving a breakthrough.

Mechanised warfare had now come to a halt. Tanks on both sides were used as little more than static pillboxes and artillery, a clear reflection of how the war had bogged down into a battle of attrition. The Chinese conducted a series of probing attacks in the New Year and in July 1952 began the 'Outposts Battles' by attacking key UN hill-top positions along the front. All these operations resulted in heavy losses, particularly for the Chinese. By the end of the year though there were 270,000 Chinese and North Korean troops, supported by 513,000 reserves, facing the UN forces.

Superior UN firepower meant that these forces were destined to be decimated. Battle recommenced in March 1953 when the Chinese attacked towards Seoul. Two more attacks were launched in the centre during the summer. The second conducted on 13 July cost the Chinese 72,000 men before the armistice on 27 July 1953 finally brought 3 years of hostilities to an end.

Although the Chinese singularly failed to employ tanks, the North Koreans continued to expand their armoured forces. By this stage of the war the NKPA consisted of almost 20 divisions, supported by 7 tank regiments, organised into 6 armies. The RoK Army had a similar number of divisions.

(*Opposite*) Major General Frank Lowe, US presidential representative, examines a Marines' range finder. By the winter of 1951 both sides were firmly dug in and neither had much hope of breaking through. During the summer of 1952 the Communists launched a series of probing attacks against UN outposts such as this, but they all resulted in heavy casualties. (*US DoD*)

Men of a 4.2in mortar crew, 31st Heavy Mortar Company, fire on enemy positions west of Chorwon, 7 February 1953. The following month the Chinese attacked towards Seoul and there then followed a year of positional warfare before the armistice was finally signed. (*Author's Collection*)

This dug-in machine-gun team is from the US 2nd Infantry Division, armour support was provided by the 72nd Tank Battalion. (*US DoD*)

This M46 Patton is being used in an indirect fire support role, hence it being parked on the high-angled earth ramp and the ammunition stacked outside the tank. (*US DoD*)

Two young Koreans pose in front of a Pershing or Patton tank. This was the pre-eminent tank type of the war. (*US DoD*)

The Communists found it difficult to contend with the UN forces' air power and artillery. The M41 howitzer motor carriage mounted a 155mm on the chassis of the M24 Chaffee light tank and was known unofficially as the 'Gorilla'. This particular gun belongs to Battery A, 92nd Armored Field Artillery Battalion and is firing near Kumhwa on 8 June 1952. (*US DoD*)

An 8in howitzer, but not self-propelled, from the 17th Field Artillery Battalion shelling Chinese positions south of Chorwon, 10 June 1951. (*US DoD*)

Another howitzer from the 96th Field Artillery Battalion firing on Communist positions near Yanggau, 25 June 1951. (*Author's Collection*)

These 90mm anti-aircraft guns are supporting the RoK 1st Infantry Division fighting north of Taegu. Communist fighter bombers never posed a real threat to UN ground forces. (*US DoD*)

Tractors of the 196th Field Artillery pulling 155mm guns. Artillery took over from tanks as the Korean War bogged down and drew to a stalemate. (*US DoD*)

Men of Battery C, 936th Field Artillery Battalion fire the 200,000th round of ammunition on 12 April 1952. Shortly afterwards the Chinese started what became known as the 'Outposts Battles'. (*US DoD*)

Members of the 81mm Mortar Platoon, Company D, US 5th Infantry Regiment drop mortar bombs onto Communist positions, 12 August 1952. (*US DoD*)

US troops are briefed from the back of an armoured vehicle. As both sides were tiring of the war, most men simply wanted to get home in one piece. (*US DoD*)

US troops taking cover. By the summer of 1953 the Korean War had ground to a complete halt and both sides acknowledged that further bloodshed would achieve nothing. By this stage of the war the NKPA had seven regiments of T-34 tanks, thanks to the armistice they did not see further action. (*US DoD*)